Herd Instinct

© Copyright Dave Karpinsky 2025. All rights reserved.

No part of this publication may be reproduced, stored in a retrieval system, or transmitted in any form or by any means—electronic, mechanical, photocopying, recording, or otherwise—without the prior written permission of the author or publisher.

The author and publisher shall not be held liable for any damages, losses, or legal claims arising directly or indirectly from the use or misuse of the information contained in this book.

Legal Notice:

This book is copyright protected. It is intended solely for personal use. No part of this publication may be sold, copied, altered, distributed, quoted, or paraphrased without express permission from the author or publisher.

Disclaimer Notice:

The contents of this book are intended for educational and entertainment purposes only. While every effort has been made to ensure accuracy, completeness, and reliability, no warranties are expressed or implied. The author is not offering legal, financial, medical, or professional advice. The information presented is based on research, experience, and publicly available sources.

Readers should consult qualified professionals before making decisions based on this material. By reading this book, you acknowledge that the author is not responsible for any loss, damage, or adverse consequences resulting from the application of the information herein, including but not limited to errors, omissions, or inaccuracies.

Other books written by Dave Karpinsky

Artificial Intelligence & Information Technology
- Artificial Intelligence (AI) for Daily Life: A Practical Guide to Artificial Intelligence
- AI and Creativity: How Machines are Changing Art, Music & Literature
- AI-Powered PM: Leveraging Artificial Intelligence for Enhanced Efficiency and Success
- Artificial Intelligence Rise and Humanity Fall
- Data-Driven Future: Harnessing AI and Big Data for Tomorrow's Challenges
- Deepfake Technology: The Dark Side of AI, Manipulation and Digital Deception.
- Fixing Failed Projects: How to Master the Art of Project Turnaround
- From Data to Decisions: The Role of AI in Business Intelligence
- Jobs AI Will Replace: Re-tool or Be Left Behind
- Mastering Advanced Project Management: Strategies for Excellence
- Mastering Project Management: In complex, stressful & high-pressure environments
- SAP S/4 Implementation: A Comprehensive Guide for Practitioners
- SAP S/4 Implementation Methodologies
- SAP S/4 Implementation – Volume 1: Prep & Explore Phases
- SAP S/4 Implementation – Volume 2: Realize & Deploy Phases
- SAP S/4 Implementation – Volume 3: When Projects Fail

- The Five-Day Organizational Change Manager
- The Five--Day Project Manager
- The Project Management Masterclass: Advanced Techniques for Success
- The Rise of Real-Time Analytics: Speed, Precision, and Competitive Edge

Business & Finance
- Building Wealth in Developing Nations: A Comprehensive Step-by-Step Guide to Empower Emerging Markets
- Chief Executive's (CxO) Playbook: The First 90 Days Guide to Success
- Creating a Deployment Plan: Navigating Complexity to Deliver Success
- Creating a Strategic Roadmap: Crafting the Blueprint from Vision to Execution
- Investing Strategies of the Rich and Famous: Discover How to Diversify Your Portfolio for Maximum Returns
- Outsmart the Game: Winning When the Rules Are Rigged
- The Data Delusion: Exposing False Metrics That Shape Your World
- Trust is the New Currency: How Connection Wins in the Age of AI

Life Coach & Mentor Series
- Aspiring Entrepreneurs
- Bored Housewife
- Career Transition
- Couples and Relationships

- Mid-Life Crisis
- Mindful Healthy Living
- Project Managers
- Seeking Life's Purpose
- Surviving Holidays with In-laws

Science & Physics
- Game Over. Reset Earth
- Quantum Entanglement: The God Effect and the Secrets of Reality
- Multiverse Parallel Dimensions: The Theories and Possibilities of Parallel Universes
- Space-Time Continuum: Navigating the Quantum of the Fourth Dimension
- The Hubble Tension: The Universe's Expansion, Cosmology Crisis, and the Limits of the Big Bang Theory
- The Singularity Shift: Unveiling the Future of Humanity and Intelligence
- Twin Paradox: Solving the Puzzle of Special Relativity

Sociology & Politics
- America at War: Russia, China, Iran, S Korea
- Blue Zones Volume 1: Mystery and Science of Blue Zones
- Blue Zones Volume 2: Longevity Lessons of Blue Zones
- Decline of American Supremacy: Understanding the Erosion, Shaping the Future
- Future of Military Technology Powered by AI: How countries are transforming their warfare

- Herd Instinct: Understanding the Human Psychology of Collective Behavior
- Preventing Squatters: A Comprehensive Guide to Protecting Your Property
- Puppet Masters: The Hidden Hands of Political Power
- The Great War of China vs Russia: A Future Battlefield that Reshapes the World
- The Modern Stoic: 365 Ancient Practices for Wisdom, Peace, Purpose ad Strength
- The Next Battlefield: How AI, Robotics, and Biotechnology are Transforming Warfare
- The Savage Guide to Winning: The Brutal Truth About Success
- The Trump Effect: Return to the White House
- The Vatican Murder Cover-Up
- Unf*k Yourself: A No-Bullsh!t Guide to Taking Control
- Warfare Redefined: Military Technologies and Tactics of Tomorrow's Superpowers
- Zero F*cks Given: How to Stop Worrying and Live Your Life
- God & AI Series:
  - Is There God: According to Artificial Intelligence (AI)
  - What is God: According to Artificial Intelligence (AI)
  - What is God's Plan: According to Artificial Intelligence (AI)

"We follow not because we trust the path, but because we fear standing alone."
— *Dave Karpinsky*

Herd Instinct

Understanding the Human Psychology of Collective Behavior

Dave Karpinsky, PhD, MBA, PMP, Prosci

Green Parrot Media

Contents

Introduction: The Unseen Force That Drives Us 15

Chapter 1: The Power of the Herd: An Overview 23

Part I: The Psychology Behind Herd Mentality 31

Chapter 2: The Evolutionary Roots of Herd Behavior 33

Chapter 3: Psychological Foundations of Conformity 41

Part II: Mechanisms and Triggers of Herd Behavior 49

Chapter 4: Cognitive Biases and Groupthink 51

Chapter 5: Media Influence and Information Cascades ... 61

Part III: The Impact of Herd Mentality 71

Chapter 6: Economic Bubbles and Financial Crashes....... 73

Chapter 7: Social Movements and Political Revolutions.. 81

Part IV: Resisting the Pull of the Herd 89

Chapter 8: The Importance of Critical Thinking 91

Conclusion 99

Chapter 9: Leadership and Influence............................. 101

Appendices 109

Appendix A: Key Terms and Concepts 111

Appendix B: Recommended Reading and Resources 117

Appendix C: Case Study Analysis.................................. 125

Introduction: The Unseen Force That Drives Us

In the heart of the African savannah, a lone zebra pauses, ears twitching, eyes scanning the horizon. The air is thick with tension, the kind that precedes a predator's strike. Suddenly, a distant movement sends a ripple through the herd. The zebras burst into motion as if on cue, galloping in unison across the plain. This scene, repeated in countless forms across the animal kingdom, is a testament to the power of collective behavior. This phenomenon has shaped the survival and success of species for millennia. But what about humans? Are we so different from the zebra, or does the same invisible force guide our actions?

Welcome to *"Herd Instinct: Understanding the Human Psychology of Collective Behavior,"* a journey into the depths of a force that has steered human history, influenced societal norms, and continues to drive our decisions today.

This book seeks to unravel the complex, often hidden, dynamics of herd mentality—a concept that has far-reaching implications for our lives, communities, and the world.

The Genesis of Collective Behavior

To genuinely understand herd instinct, we must first journey back to the origins of our species, where the seeds of collective behavior were sown. Much like the zebras of the savannah, our earliest ancestors relied on the group for survival. In a world fraught with danger, the lone individual was vulnerable, but within the tribe's safety, there was strength. This ancient need for social cohesion has left an indelible mark on our psychology, influencing our thinking, feeling, and acting in often unconscious ways.

Consider the hunter-gatherer societies of prehistoric times. Survival depended on the group's ability to work together, share resources, and protect each other from predators. Cooperation was not just beneficial—it was essential. Those who did not conform to the group's norms or who failed to contribute were at risk of being ostracized, a fate that, in those days, could be as deadly as any predator. This ingrained fear of isolation has persisted through the ages, driving us to seek the group's comfort, even when it means suppressing our judgments.

The Power of the Crowd

As humanity progressed, the power of collective behavior began to manifest in more complex forms. Ancient civilizations were built on the foundations of collective effort. The construction of the pyramids in Egypt, the Great Wall of China, and the Roman Empire's vast infrastructure were all made possible by the coordinated efforts of large groups of people driven by shared beliefs, goals, and, sometimes, fear.

One of the most striking examples of early collective behavior is the rise of religious movements. The spread of Christianity, for instance, is a testament to the power of the herd instinct. In a time of uncertainty and persecution, the early Christians found strength in numbers. Their collective belief in a common cause sustained them and helped them spread their faith across vast territories, eventually influencing entire empires.

The same force can be seen in the mass migrations that have shaped history. The great migrations of the Goths and Vandals in the late Roman Empire, the Viking invasions of Europe, and the colonization of the Americas were all driven by collective action. These movements, often spurred by environmental pressures, warfare, or economic necessity, were expressions of a deep-seated instinct to move as a group, seeking safety, resources, and a better future.

The Psychology of the Herd

But what drives this instinct? Why do individuals capable of independent thought and decision-making so often surrender to the will of the group? The answer lies in the intricate workings of the human mind.

Psychologists have long studied the phenomena of conformity and social influence, and their findings reveal that the desire to fit in is one of the most powerful motivators of human behavior. This is not simply a matter of wanting to be liked; it is about survival. The brain is wired to seek out social connections, and when faced with uncertainty, we naturally look to others for cues on how to behave. This is known as informational social influence—when people conform because they believe others have more accurate information.

However, normative social influence is also at play—the desire to be accepted and avoid social rejection. This can lead individuals to adopt behaviors or opinions they do not necessarily agree with to avoid being ostracized. These two forces, working together, create a potent cocktail that can lead to widespread conformity, even in the face of clear evidence to the contrary.

Modern Manifestations of Herd Mentality

In today's world, the influence of herd mentality is perhaps more pervasive than ever before, thanks to the advent of technology and social media. The digital age has created new platforms for collective behavior, where ideas, trends, and panics can spread lightning.
Social media platforms, in particular, have amplified the effects of herd mentality. The "likes" and "shares" on these platforms create a virtual feedback loop where individuals are rewarded for conforming to popular opinions and behaviors. This can lead to the rapid spread of misinformation, the viral nature of trends, and the formation of echo chambers, where the roar of the majority drowns out dissenting voices.

Consider the phenomenon of viral challenges — those social media trends where people mimic a specific action or behavior, often without fully understanding the context or consequences. From the harmless Ice Bucket Challenge to the more dangerous Tide Pod Challenge, these trends demonstrate how quickly herd mentality can take hold in the digital age. The desire to be part of the crowd and participate in what everyone else is doing can override individual judgment and lead to risky behavior.

In the financial world, herd mentality can lead to dramatic market fluctuations, as seen in the 2008 financial crisis and the more recent GameStop stock frenzy. In both cases, investors, driven by others' actions, made decisions based not on careful analysis but on the belief that it must be the right move if everyone else was doing it. The result? Market bubbles and crashes have far-reaching consequences for economies and individuals alike.

The Dark Side of the Herd

While herd mentality can bring people together and drive collective achievements, it also has a darker side. History is replete with examples of how the power of the herd has led to devastating outcomes, from the atrocities committed during the Holocaust to the mass suicides of cults like Jonestown. These extreme examples highlight the dangers of uncritical conformity and the potential for manipulation by charismatic leaders who understand how to exploit the herd instinct for their ends.

In these cases, the exact psychological mechanisms that promote social cohesion and group identity can be turned against individuals, leading them to commit acts they would never consider on their own. The fear of being an outsider and believing that the group knows best can suppress moral judgment and critical thinking, leading to tragic consequences.

Harnessing the Power of the Herd

Despite its potential dangers, herd mentality is not inherently harmful. It can be harnessed for positive outcomes. Social movements, for instance, rely on the power of the herd to effect change. The Civil Rights Movement, the fight for women's suffrage, and more recent movements like #MeToo have all leveraged collective behavior to challenge the status quo and push for progress.

The key to harnessing the power of the herd lies in understanding it. By recognizing the psychological forces at play, individuals and leaders can guide collective behavior in ways that promote positive outcomes while mitigating the risks of blind conformity. This requires a balance— encouraging social cohesion and collective action while fostering critical thinking and individual responsibility.

As we navigate the complexities of modern society, understanding the psychology of collective behavior is more critical than ever. The herd instinct is a powerful force that shapes our actions, decisions, and lives in ways we may not know. By exploring the dynamics of herd mentality, we can better understand ourselves and the world around us, gaining the tools to navigate the crowd with a clear sense of direction and purpose.

In the following chapters, we will delve deeper into the many facets of herd behavior, exploring its impact on history, society, and the individual. We will examine the fine line between social cohesion and mass hysteria, the role of leaders in guiding the herd, and how we can resist the pull of the crowd when it leads us astray. Through this exploration, we hope to shed light on one of the most fascinating and influential aspects of human behavior — the power of the herd.

Dave Karpinsky

Chapter 1: The Power of the Herd: An Overview

Definition of Herd Mentality

Herd mentality, often called mob mentality, is the inclination for individuals within a group to conform to the majority's behavior, beliefs, and decisions. This phenomenon is not just a curiosity about human behavior but a deeply ingrained instinct that can influence everything from consumer choices to global politics. At its core, herd mentality emerges from the human need for belonging and acceptance, often overriding individual judgment and critical thinking.

When we speak of herd mentality, we're referring to situations where people collaborate without centralized direction, often driven by emotions rather than logic. This can be seen in conditions ranging from stock market trends to social movements, and it usually leads to outcomes that no single individual would have chosen on their own. The term evokes the image of animals moving in unison — like a flock of birds or a school of fish — where the group's movement is instinctual, almost unconscious.

From an evolutionary standpoint, this behavior was essential for survival. Early humans depended on their tribes for protection and resources, and those who strayed too far from the group were vulnerable to predators. This instinctual behavior has carried over into modern times, influencing everything from how we shop to how we vote.

The fear of being left out or ostracized by the group can be a powerful motivator, leading individuals to adopt the behaviors and beliefs of the majority, often without question.

Historical Examples of Herd Behavior

To understand the full impact of herd mentality, we can look at several key historical moments where collective behavior shaped the course of events. These examples illustrate the herd's power and highlight the potential dangers of unchecked conformity.

The Madness of Crowds: The Dutch Tulip Mania of the 1630s

One of the most infamous examples of herd mentality driving economic behavior is the Dutch Tulip Mania of the early 17th century. Tulips were introduced to Europe from the Ottoman Empire in the late 1500s, and by the 1630s, they had become a symbol of wealth and status in the Dutch Republic. As demand for the flowers grew, so did their prices, leading to a speculative bubble that would later become a classic case study in economic irrationality.

The frenzy began modestly, with the wealthy seeking rare and exotic tulip bulbs as a status symbol. However, as the prices continued to rise, more people from all walks of life started investing in tulips, driven by the belief that they could resell them at a higher price. This speculative buying created a self-reinforcing cycle where the mere expectation of higher prices led to even higher prices.

At the peak of the mania, some tulip bulbs were reportedly sold for the equivalent of a skilled craftsman's annual salary or even more. However, in February 1637, the bubble burst. As prices began to fall, panic set in, and the market collapsed almost overnight, leaving many investors in financial ruin. The Tulip Mania is often cited as one of the first examples of an economic bubble driven by herd mentality, where collective optimism led to irrational behavior and, ultimately, disaster.

The Salem Witch Trials: Fear and Hysteria in Colonial America

In 1692, the small Puritan settlement of Salem, Massachusetts, became the epicenter of one of the most notorious instances of mass hysteria in American history — the Salem Witch Trials. The trials were fueled by a combination of religious fervor, fear of the unknown, and a community already on edge due to ongoing conflicts and hardship.

The hysteria began when several young girls in Salem Village claimed to be possessed by the devil and accused several local women of witchcraft. These accusations quickly spread, fueled by fear and paranoia. The trials that followed saw the execution of 20 people and the imprisonment of many more, mainly based on flimsy evidence and the power of suggestion.

The Salem Witch Trials are a cautionary tale of how herd mentality can lead to collective fear and irrational behavior. The community, driven by fear and the desire to root out evil, abandoned reason and due process. Individuals who might have had doubts were swept along by the overwhelming tide of public opinion, leading to one of the darkest chapters in early American history.

The South Sea Bubble: An Economic Lesson in Herd Mentality

The South Sea Bubble of 1720 is another classic example of herd mentality leading to economic disaster. The South Sea Company was a British joint-stock company founded in 1711, which was granted a monopoly to trade with South America. The company's stock became the subject of fevered speculation, driven by wild promises of immense profits.

As word spread of the potential riches to be made, people from all levels of society began investing in South Sea Company shares, often without understanding the company's actual business or the risks involved. The stock price skyrocketed, fueled by speculative buying and the belief that prices would only continue to rise.

However, the company's prospects were far less promising than the hype suggested. When the bubble finally burst in September 1720, the price of South Sea shares plummeted, leading to widespread financial ruin. The South Sea Bubble is a stark reminder of how herd mentality can drive individuals to make irrational decisions, mainly when fueled by the fear of missing out on potential gains.

The French Revolution: The Power of Collective Action

While many examples of herd mentality result in adverse outcomes, it can also be a force for positive change. The French Revolution, which began in 1789, is a powerful example of how collective behavior can lead to overthrowing oppressive regimes and the birth of new political systems.

The revolution was driven by widespread discontent among the French population, notably the Third Estate, which comprised most of the population but had little political power. As economic hardship and social inequality worsened, the French people demanded change. What started as isolated protests soon became a mass movement driven by the collective desire for liberty, equality, and fraternity.

The French Revolution demonstrates how herd mentality can lead to significant social and political change. The shared belief in a common cause united a diverse population, allowing them to challenge the existing power structures and create a new order. However, the revolution also highlights the potential dangers of unchecked collective behavior, as the initial push for reform eventually gave way to the Reign of Terror, where thousands were executed in the name of revolutionary justice.

Modern Manifestations of Herd Mentality

Herd mentality is not just a relic of the past; it plays a significant role in modern society. From financial markets to social media, the power of the herd can be seen in various contexts, often with profound implications.

The Dot-Com Bubble: The Internet Boom and Bust

The Dot-Com Bubble of the late 1990s is a recent example of herd mentality driving economic behavior. As the internet revolutionized how we communicate, work, and shop, investors flocked to technology stocks, particularly those associated with internet-based companies.
The belief that the internet would fundamentally change the economy led to a speculative frenzy, with investors pouring

money into companies with little or no revenue simply because they were associated with the Internet. Stock prices soared, and many investors made substantial profits — on paper. However, by the early 2000s, it became clear that many of these companies would never be profitable. The bubble burst, leading to massive losses and the collapse of many companies.

The Dot-Com Bubble illustrates how herd mentality can lead to unsustainable market behavior. It is driven by the fear of missing out and the assumption that it must be a good idea if everyone else is investing.

Social Media: The New Frontier of Herd Mentality

In the digital age, social media has become a powerful platform for expressing a herd mentality. The algorithms that power social media platforms are designed to amplify content that resonates with large groups of people, creating echo chambers where popular opinions are reinforced and dissenting voices are marginalized.

This has significant implications for everything from political discourse to consumer behavior. Viral trends, whether memes, challenges, or political movements, spread rapidly through social media, driven by the collective behavior of millions of users. The pressure to conform and be part of the conversation can lead individuals to adopt behaviors or beliefs they might not otherwise consider.

For example, the viral spread of misinformation on social media has become a significant concern in recent years.

False information can spread quickly, driven by the herd mentality of sharing content others have shared without critically evaluating its accuracy. This has had real-world consequences, from influencing elections to fueling public health crises.

Conclusion: Understanding the Power of the Herd

Herd mentality is a powerful force that has shaped human behavior throughout history and continues to do so today. By understanding the psychology behind collective behavior, we can better navigate the challenges and opportunities it presents. Whether it's in the stock market, social movements, or our everyday interactions, the influence of the herd is ever-present.

In this book, we will explore the many facets of herd mentality, examining its impact on society, culture, and the individual. We will delve into the psychological mechanisms that drive collective behavior, the historical examples that illustrate its power, and how we can harness or resist the pull of the herd in our lives. Through this exploration, we hope to shed light on one of human nature's most fascinating aspects — the herd's power.

Part I: The Psychology Behind Herd Mentality

Chapter 2: The Evolutionary Roots of Herd Behavior

Survival Instincts and Social Animals

A herd of wildebeest grazes under the relentless sun in the vast plains of the African savannah. All seems calm, but suddenly, tension spreads through the group. Without warning, the herd begins to move as one, a mass of bodies thundering across the landscape, driven by an instinct older than time. What compels these creatures to act in such perfect unison? The answer lies deep within the evolutionary roots of herd behavior — an ancient survival mechanism refined and reinforced over millennia.

Herd behavior, at its most fundamental level, is a survival strategy. Living in groups offers social animals significant advantages, particularly in environments where predators are constantly threatened. By banding together, individuals reduce the likelihood of being singled out by a predator — a concept often called the "dilution effect." When a predator approaches a large group, the probability that any individual will be attacked decreases significantly. This simple yet powerful principle has been a driving force behind the evolution of group behavior in many species, from the great herds of ungulates on the African plains to schools of fish in the ocean.

However, the benefits of herd behavior extend beyond mere safety in numbers. In a herd, individuals can also take advantage of collective vigilance. While a lone animal must constantly be alert for danger, group members can share this burden, with different individuals taking turns watching for predators. This allows the others to focus on foraging or other essential activities, ensuring they will be alerted to any threats.

The evolution of these behaviors can be traced back to the early stages of life on Earth. As the first multicellular organisms began to form, the advantages of living in groups became increasingly apparent. In the primordial oceans, simple organisms that clumped together were better able to resist environmental pressures, such as changes in temperature or salinity, than those that remained solitary. Over time, these clumps of cells became more specialized and coordinated, eventually giving rise to the complex social behaviors we see in animals today.

The Evolutionary Benefits of Group Behavior

To fully appreciate the evolutionary roots of herd behavior, it's essential to consider the broader context of social behavior in the animal kingdom. Social animals, ranging from ants to elephants, have evolved various group behaviors that enhance their survival and reproductive success. These behaviors are not just about avoiding predators; they also play a crucial role in accessing resources, raising offspring, and navigating complex environments.

Cooperative Hunting and Resource Acquisition

One of the most striking examples of the benefits of group behavior is seen in cooperative hunting. In many predator species, individuals who hunt in groups can take down prey that would be impossible to capture alone. Wolves, for example, are highly social animals that rely on coordinated pack behavior to hunt large herbivores like elk and bison. They can surround and outmaneuver their prey by working together, using tactics honed over countless generations.

Similarly, in the oceans, orcas (also known as killer whales) have developed sophisticated hunting techniques that involve cooperation among pod members. Some orcas have been observed creating waves to knock seals off ice floes, while others coordinate their movements to herd schools of fish into tight balls, making them easier to capture. These behaviors are not just the result of individual intelligence; they are deeply ingrained in the species' social structure, passed down through generations, and reinforced by the success they bring.

But cooperative behaviors benefit not just predators. Herbivores, too, have evolved group strategies to maximize their access to resources. Elephants, for example, live in matriarchal herds that provide a stable social structure for raising young and finding food. The matriarch, usually the oldest and most experienced female, leads the group to watering holes and feeding grounds, drawing on her knowledge of the landscape. This collective wisdom is vital for the herd's survival, particularly in environments where resources are scarce and dispersed.

Collective Decision-Making and Navigation

Another significant evolutionary benefit of herd behavior is the ability to make collective decisions, particularly in navigation. Many animals must travel long distances to find food, water, or suitable breeding grounds, and doing so as a group can increase the chances of success. However, coordinating the movements of a large group presents a unique set of challenges. How does a herd of thousands of wildebeest decide which direction to move? How does a flock of birds know when to change course during migration?

Research has shown that in many species, these decisions are not made by a single leader but emerge from the interactions of the individuals within the group. This process, known as "self-organization," allows groups to make complex decisions without centralized control. For example, in a migrating flock of birds, each individual follows a simple set of rules—maintain a certain distance from your neighbors, align your direction with theirs, and avoid collisions. The result is a coordinated movement that appears almost choreographed, allowing the flock to change direction rapidly and efficiently in response to environmental cues.

In some species, decision-making is more democratic. For example, honeybees use "consensus building" to choose a new nesting site. Scout bees search for potential sites and then return to the hive to "vote" by performing a dance communicating the location's quality. The more bees that dance to a particular site, the more likely the swarm will choose that location. This process ensures that the colony selects the best possible site, balancing the preferences of individual bees with the needs of the group.

Altruism and Kin Selection

One of the more puzzling aspects of group behavior is altruism—actions that benefit others at a cost to the individual performing them. In evolutionary terms, this seems counterintuitive; natural selection should favor behaviors that increase an individual's reproductive success. However, altruism is widespread in the animal kingdom, and it plays a critical role in the survival of social species.

The concept of kin selection offers a potential explanation for this behavior. The kin selection suggests that individuals can increase their genetic success by helping relatives who share many of the same genes to survive and reproduce.

This idea is encapsulated in the famous quote by evolutionary biologist J.B.S. Haldane, who quipped that he would lay down his life for "two brothers or eight cousins," reflecting the mathematical relationship of shared genetic material.

In practice, kin selection can be seen in the behavior of many social animals. For example, in meerkat colonies, individuals stand guard while others forage. The sentinel meerkat is exposed to greater danger while on duty, but protecting the group helps ensure the survival of its relatives. Similarly, sterile worker ants devote their lives to raising the queen's offspring in ant colonies, effectively sacrificing their reproductive potential for the colony's benefit.

This form of altruism, while seemingly selfless, is ultimately driven by the same evolutionary forces that shape all behavior—namely, the desire to pass on one's genes to the next generation. By ensuring the survival of close relatives, individuals can indirectly increase their genetic success, even if they do not reproduce.

The Human Connection: From Evolution to Modern Society

While much of the discussion has focused on non-human animals, it's essential to recognize that humans are also profoundly influenced by these evolutionary roots. From forming families to creating nations, our social behaviors are built on the same foundations as the animal kingdom's herds, flocks, and packs.

In early human societies, the benefits of group living were clear. Bands of hunter-gatherers who worked together to hunt, gather, and protect each other were more likely to survive and thrive. These groups shared resources, cared for each other's offspring, and developed complex social structures that allowed them to navigate the challenges of their environment.

As human societies grew in size and complexity, so too did the mechanisms of social cohesion. Cultural norms, religious beliefs, and legal systems all evolved to reinforce group behavior and ensure individual cooperation. The same instincts that once drove our ancestors to form hunting parties now influence how we organize our communities, build our economies, and govern our nations.

In modern times, these evolutionary instincts can sometimes manifest in less adaptive ways. For example, the same drive to conform that once helped our ancestors survive can now lead to the spread of harmful behaviors or ideas. Herd mentality, while beneficial in many contexts, can contribute to phenomena like groupthink, where critical thinking is sacrificed for consensus.

Conclusion: The Enduring Legacy of Evolutionary Group Behavior

The evolutionary roots of herd behavior run deep, shaping the survival strategies of animals and the social structures of human societies. From the safety in numbers provided by a herd of zebras to the cooperative hunting strategies of wolves, group behavior has been a critical factor in the success of countless species.

These ancient instincts continue to influence humans' lives profoundly. Understanding the evolutionary origins of herd behavior can help us better navigate the challenges of modern society, recognizing when to embrace the group's wisdom and strike out on our own.

As we explore the psychology of collective behavior in this book, we will delve into how herd mentality shapes our world—from the dynamics of social movements to the influence of mass media. By examining the past, we can gain valuable insights into the present and, perhaps, find new ways to harness the power of the herd for the greater good.

Chapter 3: Psychological Foundations of Conformity

Social Proof and Influence

Imagine walking down a busy street in a city you've never visited. You're hungry and looking for a place to eat. On one corner, you notice a small café with a line out the door, while another café across the street sits empty. Without knowing anything about the quality of the food, which one are you more likely to choose? If you're like most people, you'll head toward the crowded café. This decision is influenced by a powerful psychological phenomenon known as social proof, a cornerstone of conformity that has profound implications for human behavior.

Social proof is the idea that people look to the behavior of others to determine their actions, especially in situations of uncertainty. When unsure what to do, we assume that others, particularly those around us, possess more information or insight; therefore, their behavior is the correct course of action. This tendency is deeply rooted in our psychology and is a crucial driver of conformity in everyday life and critical situations.

The Power of Social Proof in Everyday Life

Social proof manifests in various aspects of daily life, often without us even realizing it. Consider how online reviews influence our purchasing decisions. When shopping for a product on Amazon, we are likelier to choose an item with hundreds of positive reviews over one with only a few, even if we know nothing about the reviewers. The sheer volume of others endorsing a product is a compelling argument for its quality, even though we have no direct evidence.

This principle also plays a significant role in social media. The number of likes, shares, or comments a post receives can influence how others perceive it. A post with thousands of likes is more likely to be seen as credible, important, or worth engaging with, regardless of its content. This is why viral trends or challenges can spread so quickly; as more people participate, the momentum builds, drawing in even more participants influenced by the actions of those before them.

But social proof doesn't just influence trivial decisions like where to eat or what to buy; it also plays a crucial role in more serious contexts, such as public safety. In an emergency, individuals often look to the behavior of others to gauge how to respond. If a fire alarm goes off in a building, but no one else appears concerned or is evacuating, individuals may hesitate to act, assuming others know something they don't. This can lead to dangerous delays in responding to real threats.

Historical Examples of Social Proof in Action

The concept of social proof is not new; history is replete with examples where the behavior of the masses has influenced individual actions, sometimes with significant consequences.

The Asch Conformity Experiments

Psychologist Solomon Asch conducted one of the most famous studies demonstrating the power of social proof in the 1950s. Asch wanted to explore how much social pressure from a majority group could influence an individual to conform, even when the group was wrong.

In his experiments, participants were asked to complete a simple task: identify which of three comparison lines matched the length of a standard line. The correct answer was obvious. However, in a group setting where the other participants (who were confederates of the experimenter) deliberately chose the wrong line, many participants conformed to the group's incorrect choice despite the evidence of their own eyes.

Asch's experiments revealed that a significant percentage of people would conform to the majority opinion, even when it was blatantly incorrect, highlighting the powerful influence of social proof. These findings have had lasting implications for our understanding of conformity and have been replicated in various forms across different cultures and contexts.

The Jonestown Massacre

A more tragic example of social proof in action is the Jonestown Massacre of 1978, where over 900 members of the Peoples Temple, a cult led by Jim Jones, died in a mass suicide in the jungles of Guyana. While many factors contributed to this horrific event, social proof played a critical role in the final hours of the group's existence.

Under immense pressure and in a highly controlled environment, individuals looked to the behavior of others to guide their actions. As some members began to drink the poisoned Kool-Aid, others followed suit, even those who may have had doubts or fears. The group's behavior provided a powerful signal that influenced individual decisions, leading to one of modern society's most devastating examples of conformity.

The Role of Fear and Uncertainty

If social proof is the carrot that drives conformity, fear and uncertainty are the sticks. When people are afraid or uncertain, they are even more likely to conform to the behavior of others, seeking safety in numbers and reassurance in the collective.

Fear as a Catalyst for Conformity

Fear is a primal emotion, deeply embedded in our psyche, designed to protect us from danger. When faced with a physical, social, or psychological threat, our natural response is to seek safety. In many cases, that safety is found in the group. Conforming to the behavior of others can reduce the perceived threat, as it suggests that the group's actions are a means of survival.

One of the most powerful demonstrations of this dynamic is seen in wartime propaganda and the rise of totalitarian regimes. In the early 20th century, both Nazi Germany and Stalinist Russia used fear as a tool to enforce conformity. Propaganda created a sense of external and internal threats—whether from political enemies, ethnic groups, or ideological opponents. The pervasive atmosphere of fear drove people to conform to the prevailing ideology, often at the expense of their own moral beliefs.

During the Holocaust, for example, many ordinary Germans and citizens of occupied countries participated in or disregarded atrocities, driven by a combination of fear, uncertainty, and social pressure. The fear of being labeled a dissenter or traitor and the uncertainty of what might happen if one did not conform led to widespread collaboration in one of history's greatest crimes.

The Power of Uncertainty

Uncertainty, like fear, is a powerful driver of conformity. When people are unsure what to do or think, they often look to others for cues. This is particularly true in novel or ambiguous situations with no clear right or wrong course of action.

A classic example of this is the phenomenon of bystander apathy, where individuals are less likely to help a victim in an emergency if other people are present. This was famously demonstrated in the case of Kitty Genovese, a young woman who was murdered in New York City in 1964 while reportedly 38 witnesses looked on without intervening. Although the case's specifics have been debated, the incident highlighted how uncertainty in a crowd can lead to inaction. Each person may have assumed that someone else would step in or that the situation was not as severe as it seemed, leading to a tragic outcome.

Uncertainty also plays a significant role in financial markets. During economic crises, such as the 2008 financial meltdown, uncertainty about the stability of banks and investments led to panic selling and a rush to withdraw funds. This herd behavior exacerbated the crisis, as individuals, uncertain about the future, followed the actions of others, leading to a downward spiral.

Harnessing Social Proof and Managing Fear

Understanding the psychological foundations of conformity—social proof, fear, and uncertainty—provides valuable insights into how we can manage and harness these forces for positive outcomes.

Social Proof for Positive Change

Social proof can be a powerful tool for encouraging positive behaviors. For instance, public health campaigns often leverage social proof by highlighting the number of people who have adopted healthy behavior, such as quitting smoking or getting vaccinated. By emphasizing the widespread acceptance of these behaviors, these campaigns create a sense of social pressure to conform to positive norms.

Another example is the use of social proof in environmental initiatives. Campaigns highlighting how many people are reducing their carbon footprint or participating in recycling programs can motivate others to follow suit. The key is to create a perception that these behaviors are expected and desirable, leveraging the natural human tendency to conform to the group.

Managing Fear and Uncertainty

On the other hand, managing fear and uncertainty is crucial in preventing harmful herd behavior. Leaders in government, business, or community organizations must know how their actions and communications can influence public perception.

Clear, consistent, and transparent communication is essential to reduce uncertainty and prevent panic during crises. Providing accurate information and outlining concrete steps individuals can take to protect themselves can help mitigate the spread of fear and reduce the likelihood of irrational herd behavior.

In financial markets, regulators and policymakers can help stabilize markets by implementing safeguards that reduce uncertainty and prevent panic selling. For example, circuit breakers that temporarily halt trading during sharp market declines can stop behavior from spiraling out of control.

Conclusion: The Dual Edges of Conformity

The psychological foundations of conformity — social proof, fear, and uncertainty — are deeply intertwined with our nature as social beings. These forces can drive both positive and negative behaviors, shaping everything from consumer choices to social movements and even the outcomes of crises.

As we navigate a world increasingly connected and influenced by others' behavior, understanding these psychological underpinnings becomes more important than ever by recognizing when we are influenced by social proof, acknowledging the role of fear and uncertainty in our decisions, and consciously choosing when to conform and stand apart, we can make more informed, intentional choices in our lives.

In the following chapters, we will explore the complex interplay of psychology and behavior, delving into how these forces shape our societies, economies, and futures. As we do, we will uncover how we can harness the herd's power for good while safeguarding against its potential dangers.

Part II: Mechanisms and Triggers of Herd Behavior

Chapter 4: Cognitive Biases and Groupthink

In 1961, a group of brilliant and experienced men gathered in a room to discuss the feasibility of a covert operation that would later become one of the most notorious failures in U.S. history—the Bay of Pigs invasion. Despite their collective expertise, the group decided to proceed with a plan that, in retrospect, was doomed to fail. How could such a group make such a flawed decision? The answer lies in a psychological phenomenon known as groupthink, heavily influenced by cognitive biases that distort our thinking and decision-making processes. This chapter will explore the cognitive biases frequently manifest in herd behavior and examine case studies where groupthink led to catastrophic outcomes.

Common Cognitive Biases in Herd Behavior

Cognitive biases are systematic patterns of deviation from rationality in judgment. They occur because our brains rely on mental shortcuts—heuristics—to process information quickly. While these shortcuts can be helpful, they often lead to errors in thinking, mainly when the behavior or opinions of others influence us. In herd behavior, several cognitive biases play a pivotal role.

Confirmation Bias

Confirmation bias is the tendency to search for, interpret, and remember information that confirms our pre-existing beliefs or hypotheses while giving disproportionately less consideration to alternative possibilities. When individuals within a group share similar beliefs or expectations, confirmation bias can reinforce them, leading the group to become more entrenched in their views, even in the face of contradictory evidence.

For example, during the lead-up to the Iraq War in 2003, confirmation bias played a significant role in the U.S. government's decision-making process. Intelligence reports that suggested Iraq had weapons of mass destruction were accepted without sufficient scrutiny, while evidence to the contrary was downplayed or ignored. This bias contributed to the decision to invade Iraq, a move that had far-reaching consequences.

Bandwagon Effect

The bandwagon effect is the tendency for individuals to adopt certain behaviors, styles, or attitudes simply because others are doing so. This bias is particularly potent in uncertain situations, as people often look to others for cues on acting. The more people adopt a specific behavior, the more likely others are to follow suit, creating a self-reinforcing cycle.

In financial markets, the bandwagon effect can lead to bubbles, where asset prices rise rapidly as more investors buy in, believing that prices will continue to increase. The dot-com bubble of the late 1990s is a prime example. Investors poured money into internet-related companies with little regard for their business models or profitability simply because others were doing the same. When the bubble burst, many lost significant amounts of money.

Herd Instinct

Closely related to the bandwagon effect, herd instinct is the tendency for individuals to follow the majority, often without critical analysis. Herd instinct is deeply rooted in our evolutionary past, where following the group was usually a matter of survival. However, this instinct can lead to irrational and sometimes dangerous behaviors in modern society.

A classic example of herd instinct is seen in stock market crashes, where panic selling occurs as investors see others sell off their assets and rush to do the same to avoid potential losses. This collective behavior can exacerbate market downturns, turning what might have been a minor correction into a full-blown crash.

Anchoring Bias

Anchoring bias occurs when individuals rely too heavily on the first piece of information they receive (the "anchor") when making decisions. This bias can significantly impact group decision-making, particularly when the initial information sets the tone for the discussion.

During the Cuban Missile Crisis in 1962, the U.S. government was initially anchored by the belief that any Soviet missiles in Cuba posed an immediate and intolerable threat. This anchoring led to heightened tensions and brought the world to the brink of nuclear war. It was only after careful deliberation and the willingness to consider alternative perspectives that the crisis was peacefully resolved.

Availability Heuristic

The availability heuristic is a mental shortcut that relies on immediate examples that come to mind when evaluating a situation. This bias can lead individuals to overestimate the importance or likelihood of more easily recalled events, often due to recent exposure or emotional impact.

In the context of herd behavior, the availability heuristic can cause people to disproportionately fear or react to situations widely reported in the media. For example, during the 2014 Ebola outbreak, fear spread rapidly in the United States even though the actual risk of contracting the disease was shallow. The intense media coverage made the threat seem more immediate and widespread than it was, leading to unnecessary panic and overreaction.

Case Studies on Groupthink

Groupthink is a psychological phenomenon within a group — the desire for harmony or conformity results in an irrational or dysfunctional decision-making outcome. Group members often suppress dissenting opinions, fail to analyze alternatives critically, and ultimately make decisions that are not in the best interest of the group or the broader society. Below, we explore two significant case studies where groupthink led to disastrous consequences.

The Bay of Pigs Invasion

In April 1961, the U.S. government launched a covert operation to overthrow Fidel Castro's government in Cuba, an event that would become known as the Bay of Pigs invasion. The operation was a catastrophic failure, leading to the capture or death of nearly all the U.S.-backed Cuban exiles involved in the invasion.

The decision-making process leading up to the invasion was marred by groupthink. President John F. Kennedy's inner circle, consisting of top advisors and military officials, became insulated from outside criticism. The group was highly cohesive, and dissenting opinions were either not voiced or dismissed. The operation's risks were downplayed, and the assumption that the Cuban population would rise against Castro—a vital premise of the plan—went unchallenged.

In hindsight, the operation was flawed from the start. Yet, the group's desire to maintain unanimity and support for Kennedy led to a collective failure to assess the plan critically. The Bay of Pigs invasion is a cautionary tale of how groupthink can lead even the most capable individuals to disastrous decisions.

The Challenger Disaster

On January 28, 1986, the space shuttle Challenger disintegrated 73 seconds after liftoff, killing all seven crew members aboard. The disaster was later attributed to the failure of an O-ring seal in one of the rocket boosters, which allowed hot gases to escape and ignite the fuel tank.

Despite engineers' concerns about the O-rings' performance in cold weather, the decision to launch Challenger was influenced by groupthink within NASA and its contractors. Pressure to maintain the launch schedule, combined with a belief in the infallibility of the shuttle program, led to the dismissal of legitimate safety concerns.

Engineers at Morton Thiokol, the contractor responsible for the solid rocket boosters, initially recommended delaying the launch due to the forecasted cold temperatures. However, the engineers' concerns were downplayed under pressure from NASA officials and company management, who were eager to proceed with the launch. The group ultimately agreed to go ahead with the launch despite the risks.

The Challenger disaster is a stark reminder of the dangers of groupthink in high-stakes situations. The desire to avoid conflict, maintain the schedule, and adhere to the belief that "NASA knows best" led to a fatal decision that could have been avoided with more open and critical discussion.

Avoiding Cognitive Biases and Groupthink

Understanding cognitive biases and groupthink mechanisms is the first step in mitigating their impact. Here are some strategies individuals and groups can use to avoid falling into these psychological traps.

Encouraging Dissent and Critical Thinking

One of the most effective ways to prevent groupthink is to encourage dissent and critical thinking within a group. Leaders should actively seek out alternative viewpoints and create an environment where team members feel comfortable voicing their concerns, even if they go against the majority opinion. This can be achieved by assigning a "devil's advocate" role within the group or by holding anonymous voting on critical decisions.

In the business world, companies like Amazon have institutionalized dissent through practices such as the "disagree and commit" approach, where employees are encouraged to express their disagreements with a decision before committing to it once the decision is made. This practice helps ensure that all perspectives are considered, reducing the likelihood of groupthink.

Diverse Teams and Independent Input

Diversity within a decision-making group can also help counteract cognitive biases and groupthink. When team members come from different backgrounds, have varied expertise, and hold diverse perspectives, they are less likely to fall into the trap of unanimous but flawed thinking. Additionally, seeking independent input from external sources can provide a fresh perspective and help identify potential blind spots.

For example, the success of the Manhattan Project during World War II, which developed the first nuclear weapons, can be partially attributed to the diversity of its team members, who came from a wide range of scientific disciplines and nationalities. This diversity fostered a rigorous debate and critical analysis culture, crucial in solving their complex problems.

Structured Decision-Making Processes

Implementing structured decision-making processes can also help reduce the influence of cognitive biases. Techniques such as Edward de Bono's "Six Thinking Hats" method encourage group members to approach problems from multiple perspectives, ensuring that all aspects of a decision are considered. Another approach uses decision matrices, where different options are evaluated against criteria, helping minimize individual biases' impact.

Structured decision-making frameworks have been advocated in public policy as a crucial tool to enhance the quality of governmental decisions. By systematically evaluating the potential outcomes of different policy options, decision-makers can reduce the risk of cognitive biases leading to suboptimal choices.

Conclusion: Navigating the Complexities of Cognitive Biases and Groupthink

Understanding cognitive biases and groupthink is crucial in making informed and rational decisions. These psychological phenomena often lead to flawed outcomes, as seen in the Bay of Pigs invasion and the Challenger shuttle disaster. However, individuals and groups can make more informed and rational decisions by working to counteract these biases.

The strategies to combat these influences are evident: Fostering an environment that encourages dissent, embracing diversity within teams, and implementing structured decision-making processes are all essential to mitigating the risks associated with cognitive biases and groupthink. By doing so, we can harness the group's collective power while ensuring that critical thinking and rational analysis are not sacrificed.

As we continue to explore the psychology of collective behavior in this book, it is essential to recognize that while the herd instinct and the drive to conform are deeply ingrained in human nature, they are not immutable. With awareness, education, and the right tools, we can navigate these complexities more effectively, leading to better decisions, stronger communities, and a more resilient society. The following chapters will delve deeper into how these principles apply in various contexts, from social movements to corporate environments, and explore ways to leverage the power of the herd for positive change.

Chapter 5: Media Influence and Information Cascades

The Role of Mass Media and Social Media

In an age where information travels faster than ever, mass media and social media play pivotal roles in shaping public opinion, spreading information, and driving collective behavior. From the momentous events of the Arab Spring, fueled by social media, to the pervasive influence of 24-hour news cycles, the media has become the engine that drives many aspects of modern life. But with this power comes responsibility—and risk.

Mass media, which includes television, radio, newspapers, and online news outlets, has historically been the primary channel through which people receive information. For decades, news anchors, journalists, and broadcasters could shape public discourse, often framing stories that align with particular narratives or agendas. The power of mass media lies not just in its reach but in its ability to present information as fact, which can then influence the beliefs and actions of millions.

Social media, however, has added a new dimension to the media landscape. Unlike traditional media, where information flows in one direction—from the source to the audience—social media enables a bidirectional flow of information, where users can share, comment, and create content. Platforms like Facebook, Twitter, Instagram, and

TikTok have democratized information dissemination, allowing anyone with an internet connection to become a broadcaster in their own right.

But this democratization comes with significant consequences. The sheer volume of information available on social media, combined with the algorithms that prioritize content based on engagement rather than accuracy, can create echo chambers where misinformation spreads rapidly. In this environment, the lines between fact, opinion, and outright falsehood become increasingly blurred, leading to the phenomenon known as information cascades.

The Mechanics of Information Cascades

An information cascade occurs when people make decisions based on the observations or actions of others rather than on their independent analysis. This phenomenon is particularly prevalent in situations where individuals have limited information and must rely on the behavior of others to make judgments. As more people follow suit, the cascade builds, often leading to widespread adoption of beliefs or behaviors that may be unfounded or even false.

To understand how information cascades work, imagine a scenario where several people are trying to decide whether to eat at one of two restaurants in a new city. The first person sees a few people entering Restaurant A and follows them, assuming they know something good about it. The following person, seeing a growing crowd at Restaurant A, also decides to join, and so on. Eventually, despite

Restaurant B being equally good or even better, it remains empty because everyone has chosen to follow the crowd. This is an example of how information cascades can lead to suboptimal outcomes.

In the digital age, information cascades are amplified by social media's speed and reach. A single tweet or post can go viral within minutes, reaching millions of people who may share it without verifying its accuracy. As part of the audience, it's crucial to take responsibility and verify the information before sharing it to prevent the spread of misinformation and its potential adverse effects.

Historical Examples of Media Influence and Information Cascades

Throughout history, the media has shaped public perception and influenced events. The power of media to create information cascades can be seen in both positive and negative contexts.

The War of the Worlds Broadcast

One of the most famous early examples of media-induced panic occurred on October 30, 1938, when Orson Welles and his Mercury Theatre on the Air broadcast a radio adaptation of H.G. Wells' novel *The War of the Worlds*. Presented as a series of news bulletins, the broadcast described a fictional Martian invasion of Earth. Despite repeated disclaimers that the program was fictional, many listeners believed the events were actual, leading to widespread panic.

This incident highlights the power of media to influence public perception, mainly when information is scarce or ambiguous. It's a reminder of the importance of critical thinking and independent judgment, especially when the truth is not immediately apparent. The panic induced by the broadcast resulted from an information cascade, where individuals, influenced by the reactions of others, came to believe in the reality of the invasion despite a lack of concrete evidence.

The Arab Spring

Fast forward to the 21st century, and the role of media—particularly social media—in shaping events is even more pronounced. The Arab Spring, a series of anti-government protests and uprisings spread across the Middle East and North Africa in 2010-2011, is a prime example of how social media can fuel information cascades and drive collective action.

Platforms like Facebook and Twitter were instrumental in organizing protests, sharing news, and galvanizing support for the movements. Social media allowed activists to bypass state-controlled media, spreading information quickly and widely. The rapid dissemination of images and stories of protests in one country inspired similar actions in others, creating a cascade effect that led to significant political change in the region.

However, social media's role in the Arab Spring also highlights the challenges of information cascades. As events unfolded at breakneck speed, the spread of accurate and inaccurate information influenced the course of the uprisings. In some cases, misinformation led to miscalculations and unintended consequences, illustrating the double-edged sword of social media's power.

The GameStop Short Squeeze

In early 2021, the financial world was rocked by an unprecedented event primarily driven by social media: the GameStop short squeeze. Organized on the subreddit r/WallStreetBets, thousands of retail investors coordinated to buy shares of GameStop, a struggling video game retailer, to drive up its stock price and squeeze out hedge funds that had heavily shorted the stock.

The event quickly became a media sensation, with headlines about the "David vs. Goliath" battle between retail investors and Wall Street dominating the news. As more people learned about the movement through social media and traditional media outlets, they joined in, further driving up the stock price. The resulting information cascade led to massive volatility in the stock market, with GameStop's stock price soaring from around $20 in early January 2021 to over $400 at its peak.

The GameStop saga is a modern example of how information cascades can influence financial markets. The rapid spread of information — and misinformation — on social media created a feedback loop where more and more people jumped on the bandwagon, not necessarily based on rational analysis but on the belief that others knew something they didn't.

The Role of Algorithms in Amplifying Information Cascades

One of the most significant factors that differentiate modern information cascades from those of the past is the role of algorithms in shaping the information we see. Social media platforms use complex algorithms to determine what content appears in users' feeds, prioritizing posts likely to generate engagement — likes, shares, comments — over those merely informative.

These algorithms create echo chambers, where users are exposed primarily to content that reinforces their existing beliefs. As a result, information cascades within these echo chambers can become self-reinforcing, with little to no counterbalance from alternative perspectives. This can lead to the rapid spread of misinformation, as false or misleading content that generates high engagement is more likely to be amplified.

For example, during the COVID-19 pandemic, misinformation about the virus, treatments, and vaccines spread rapidly on social media, often outpacing the efforts of public health officials to correct it. The algorithms prioritizing sensational or controversial content over factual information contributed to this problem, as posts that provoked solid emotional responses were more likely to go viral.

How Information Spreads and Influences

It's essential to examine the psychological mechanisms that drive our interactions with media to understand how information spreads and influences behavior. Several factors contribute to the spread of information and the formation of information cascades.

Emotion and Virality

Emotion is crucial in determining which information spreads and which does not. Content eliciting solid emotional responses — positive or negative — is more likely to be shared. This is why sensational headlines, heartwarming stories, and controversial opinions often go viral, while more measured or neutral content does not.

Research has shown that emotions such as anger, fear, and outrage are particularly effective at driving engagement on social media. These emotions create a sense of urgency, compelling users to share content quickly and widely. As a result, information that taps into these emotions can spread rapidly, influencing public opinion and behavior.

The Power of Narratives

Narratives, or stories, are another powerful tool for spreading information. Humans are naturally drawn to stories, which help us make sense of the world and our place in it. When information is presented as a compelling narrative, it is more likely to be remembered, shared, and believed.

For example, during political campaigns, candidates and their supporters often use narratives to frame issues in ways that resonate with voters. A candidate might tell a story about a struggling family to highlight the need for economic reform or use a personal anecdote to build empathy and trust. These narratives can be more persuasive than statistics or policy details, as they appeal to the emotions and values of the audience.

The Spiral of Silence

The spiral of silence is a social phenomenon in which individuals who perceive their opinions to be in the minority are less likely to express them. This leads to a false consensus that reinforces the dominance of the majority view. This can significantly impact the spread of information, as dissenting voices are silenced and the majority narrative becomes more entrenched.

The fear of backlash or social ostracism can exacerbate the spiral of silence on social media. Users may be reluctant to share opinions that differ from the prevailing narrative within their social circles, leading to a homogenization of viewpoints. This can create the illusion of consensus, even in situations where there is significant disagreement.

Conclusion: Navigating the Media Landscape in the Age of Information Cascades

In today's digital era, navigating the media landscape requires a nuanced understanding of how information spreads and influences collective behavior. Information cascades, driven by mass and social media's speed and reach, can significantly impact public opinion and decision-making. As information flows rapidly through these channels, it becomes increasingly difficult to discern fact from fiction and truth from manipulation.

To effectively navigate this landscape, individuals must develop critical media literacy skills—tools that help them analyze and evaluate the information they encounter. This includes questioning the sources of information, recognizing the emotional triggers used in the content, and being aware of cognitive biases that can cloud judgment.

Moreover, media platforms, mainly social media giants whose algorithms often prioritize engagement over accuracy, need to be more transparent and accountable. These platforms play a crucial role in shaping the information environment, and as such, they bear responsibility for curbing the spread of misinformation and promoting informed discourse.

Ultimately, while the power of media and the phenomenon of information cascades present challenges, they also offer opportunities for positive change. By fostering a more informed and critical public, we can harness the benefits of instant communication and global connectivity while mitigating the risks of misinformation and herd behavior. The key lies in a balanced approach that embraces the speed and reach of modern media but with a vigilant eye on the integrity and accuracy of the information that fuels it.

Part III: The Impact of Herd Mentality

Chapter 6: Economic Bubbles and Financial Crashes

When the stock market crashed on October 29, 1929, millions of Americans watched their life savings evaporate in hours. This event, known as Black Tuesday, marked the beginning of the Great Depression, a period of unprecedented economic hardship. But the seeds of this disaster were sown long before the crash, in the irrational exuberance and speculative frenzy that gripped the financial markets in the years leading up to it. The story of the 1929 crash is just one example of how herd behavior in financial markets can lead to economic bubbles—and, ultimately, financial crashes. This chapter explores the dynamics of herd behavior in financial markets and examines case studies of some of history's most infamous economic bubbles.

The Herd Behavior in Financial Markets

Financial markets are, by their very nature, susceptible to herd behavior. Unlike physical markets, where buyers and sellers exchange goods and services, financial markets trade in expectations, perceptions, and sentiments. These intangible factors are highly influenced by the behavior of others, leading to situations where investors collectively drive asset prices far beyond their intrinsic value—a phenomenon known as an economic bubble.

Several psychological factors drive herd behavior in financial markets. One of the most prominent is the fear of missing out or FOMO. When investors see others making significant gains in a particular asset or market, they are often compelled to join in, fearing they will miss out on potential profits. This leads to a self-reinforcing cycle where rising prices attract more investors, which drives prices even higher.

Another contributing factor is the bandwagon effect, where individuals adopt certain behaviors simply because others do. In financial markets, this can manifest as a rush to buy or sell assets based on the actions of others rather than on independent analysis or rational decision-making. As more people jump on the bandwagon, the momentum builds, and the bubble grows.

Social proof also plays a significant role in herd behavior. Investors often look to the actions of respected or successful individuals as a guide for their own decisions. When influential figures in finance, such as prominent hedge fund managers or investment analysts, endorse a particular stock or asset class, others are likely to follow suit, further fueling the bubble.

However, the very forces that drive the growth of an economic bubble also contribute to its eventual collapse. Once the bubble reaches a certain point, the market becomes increasingly unstable. Investors realize that prices are unsustainable and start selling off their holdings to lock in profits. This triggers a cascade of selling, leading to a sharp price decline and, in many cases, a full-blown market crash.

Case Studies of Economic Bubbles

History is replete with examples of economic bubbles, each driven by a unique set of circumstances but all characterized by the same underlying dynamics of herd behavior and irrational exuberance. Below, we explore some of the most notable examples.

Tulip Mania (1630s)

One of the earliest recorded instances of an economic bubble occurred in the Dutch Republic during the 1630s, in what is now known as Tulip Mania. At the height of this speculative frenzy, the price of a single tulip bulb soared to extraordinary levels, driven by a combination of rarity, novelty, and the social status associated with owning the most prized varieties.

Introduced to Europe from the Ottoman Empire, the tulip quickly became a status symbol among the Dutch elite. As demand for these exotic flowers grew, so did their prices. Speculators entered the market, buying and selling tulip bulbs to make a profit. The market became increasingly speculative, with contracts for future delivery of tulip bulbs—known as "futures"—trading at prices far higher than the actual bulbs.

At the peak of Tulip Mania, in February 1637, some tulip bulbs were reportedly selling for more than ten times the annual income of a skilled craftsman. However, the bubble burst just as quickly as it had formed. As buyers began to question the sustainability of such high prices, confidence evaporated, and the market collapsed. Within weeks, tulip prices had plummeted, leaving many investors in financial ruin. Tulip Mania is a cautionary tale of how speculative bubbles, fueled by herd behavior, can lead to devastating economic consequences.

The South Sea Bubble (1720)

The South Sea Bubble of 1720 is another classic example of herd behavior leading to an economic bubble and subsequent financial crash. The South Sea Company was a British joint-stock company granted a monopoly on trade with South America. Even though the company's actual trading prospects were limited, its stock became the subject of fevered speculation.

Lured by promises of immense profits, investors began buying shares in the South Sea Company, driving the stock price to extraordinary heights. The company's directors and other insiders, aware of the speculative frenzy, took advantage of the situation by selling their shares at inflated prices. The bubble grew as more and more investors poured their money into the company.

However, the bubble burst in September 1720 when it became clear that the company's profits would not justify the inflated stock prices. As confidence in the South Sea Company evaporated, investors rushed to sell their shares, leading to a sharp price decline. The collapse of the South Sea Bubble left many investors, including prominent members of British society, financially ruined. The scandal also led to significant political fallout and the introduction of new regulations aimed at preventing such speculative manias in the future.

The Dot-Com Bubble (1990s)

The late 1990s witnessed the rise of the Internet and the subsequent dot-com bubble, one of the most significant economic bubbles of the 20th century. As the Internet revolutionized communication, commerce, and entertainment, investors rushed to buy shares in technology companies, particularly those associated with the burgeoning Internet sector.

Venture capital poured into dot-com startups, many with little more than a website and a vague business plan. Stock prices for these companies soared, often based on the expectation of future profitability rather than actual earnings. The NASDAQ Composite Index, which included many technology stocks, surged from around 1,000 points in 1995 to over 5,000 points by March 2000.

The dot-com bubble was fueled by FOMO, the bandwagon effect, and the belief that the internet represented a new economic paradigm where traditional valuation metrics no longer applied. However, as the bubble inflated, it became increasingly clear that many of these companies were not generating the profits to justify their high valuations.

The bubble burst in March 2000 when the NASDAQ began to decline sharply. Over the next two years, the index lost nearly 80% of its value, wiping out trillions of dollars in market capitalization. Many dot-com companies went bankrupt, and the downturn affected the broader economy. The dot-com bubble serves as a reminder of the dangers of irrational exuberance and the importance of evaluating investments based on fundamentals rather than hype.

The 2008 Housing Bubble and Financial Crisis

The 2008 financial crisis, one of the most severe economic downturns since the Great Depression, was precipitated by a housing bubble that had been building for years. The roots of the crisis can be traced to a combination of factors, including easy access to credit, low interest rates, and the widespread belief that housing prices would continue to rise indefinitely.

During the early 2000s, banks and mortgage lenders began offering increasingly risky loans to borrowers, including those with poor credit histories. These subprime mortgages were often bundled and sold as mortgage-backed securities (MBS) to investors attracted by the high returns. As housing prices rose, more people bought homes, increasing prices and creating a self-reinforcing cycle.

Herd behavior played a significant role in the housing bubble, as homebuyers, real estate investors, and financial institutions all acted on the belief that housing prices would never decline. This belief was further reinforced by the actions of others, creating an information cascade that drove the bubble to unsustainable levels.

The bubble burst in 2007, when housing prices began to decline, leading to a wave of mortgage defaults. The value of mortgage-backed securities plummeted, causing massive losses for financial institutions and triggering a global financial crisis. The 2008 financial crisis had a profound global impact, resulting in widespread economic hardship, including millions of foreclosures, high unemployment, and a deep recession.

Conclusion: The Importance of Learning from the Past

Economic bubbles and financial crashes are recurring phenomena in the history of financial markets. The same underlying forces of herd behavior, speculation, and irrational exuberance drive them. While the specifics of each bubble may differ, the psychological and social dynamics fuel them remain consistent.

Understanding these dynamics is crucial for investors, policymakers, and the general public. Recognizing the signs of an inflating bubble—such as rapidly rising asset prices, speculative behavior, and widespread belief in the "new paradigm," for example—can mitigate the risks and avoid the devastating consequences that often follow.

However, history has shown that the allure of quick profits and the fear of missing out can be powerful motivators, leading even the most rational individuals to join the herd. As we navigate the complexities of financial markets, we must remain vigilant, question prevailing narratives, and make decisions based on careful analysis rather than following the crowd.

In the following chapters, we will explore the broader implications of herd behavior in other areas of society, from politics to culture, and examine how understanding these dynamics can help us build more resilient and informed communities.

Chapter 7: Social Movements and Political Revolutions

When the world witnessed the fall of the Berlin Wall in 1989, the event symbolized not just the collapse of a physical barrier but the end of a deeply entrenched political regime. The massive, peaceful demonstrations that led to this momentous event resulted from a powerful social movement driven by collective action and a shared desire for change. This chapter delves into the dynamics of herd mentality within social and political contexts, exploring how collective behavior can spark social movements and political revolutions, particularly during war and turbulence. Through historical examples, we will see how the power of the herd has shaped the course of history.

Herd Mentality in Social and Political Contexts

Social movements and political revolutions are often born from a collective sense of injustice or the desire for change. Herd mentality plays a crucial role in these contexts, as individuals who might feel powerless are encouraged when they see others taking a stand. This collective behavior can transform a group of like-minded individuals into a powerful force capable of challenging established systems and effecting significant societal change.

Several vital factors drive herd mentality in social and political contexts. The first is the shared belief in a common cause. When a large group believes in the same ideals or goals, they are more likely to come together to push for change. This shared belief is often reinforced by the actions of others within the group, creating a feedback loop where each participant's involvement strengthens the resolve of others.

Another factor is the perception of strength in numbers. Individuals who might be hesitant to act alone are often motivated to join a movement when they see others doing so. This is particularly true in environments where dissent is dangerous or discouraged, such as authoritarian regimes. The presence of others who share the same goals provides a sense of safety and legitimacy, encouraging more people to join the cause.

Finally, social movements and political revolutions are often catalyzed by the actions of charismatic leaders who can articulate the people's grievances and mobilize them toward a common goal. These leaders usually become symbols of the movement, rallying others around their vision for change.

Herd Mentality during War and Turbulence

The dynamics of herd mentality are particularly pronounced during periods of war and turbulence when societies are under immense stress and individuals search for stability. In such times, people are more likely to align themselves with groups that promise security, whether supporting a revolutionary cause or rallying behind a wartime leader.

During the war, herd mentality can manifest in various ways, from mobilizing entire populations for military efforts to the widespread acceptance of propaganda. Governments often exploit this tendency by using mass media and propaganda to shape public opinion, fostering a sense of national unity and purpose. This can lead to the rapid spread of militaristic or nationalistic sentiments, even among those who might have been more hesitant under normal circumstances.

Turbulent periods, such as economic crises or political upheaval, also amplify herd behavior. In such times, the fear of instability drives people to seek out groups or movements that offer a clear path forward, even if that path involves radical change. This was evident during the Great Depression, when economic despair fueled the rise of extremist movements across Europe, ultimately leading to World War II.

Examples from History

To understand the profound impact of herd mentality in social and political contexts, it is essential to examine historical examples where collective behavior led to significant societal change. Below, we explore three pivotal moments in history that demonstrate the power of the herd in shaping social movements and political revolutions.

The French Revolution (1789-1799)

The French Revolution is one of the most iconic examples of how herd mentality can drive a society to overthrow an established order. The revolution was fueled by widespread dissatisfaction with the monarchy, economic hardship, and a growing belief in Enlightenment ideals such as liberty, equality, and fraternity.

In the years leading up to the revolution, France was mired in an economic crisis, with a bankrupt government and widespread hunger among the population. The monarchy's inability to address these issues led to growing unrest, particularly among the Third Estate, which comprised the vast majority of the population but had little political power.

The storming of the Bastille on July 14, 1789, is often cited as the event that ignited the revolution. However, this defiance resulted from years of building tension and the collective belief that the old regime was no longer legitimate. As the revolution gained momentum, more people joined the cause, driven by the perception that the time for change had come.

The revolution ultimately led to the fall of the monarchy, the rise of the French Republic, and a period of radical social and political change. However, it also descended into chaos and violence, culminating in the Reign of Terror, during which thousands were executed under the guillotine. The French Revolution demonstrates the power and dangers of herd mentality in driving political change.

The Civil Rights Movement (1950s-1960s)

The Civil Rights Movement in the United States is a powerful example of how herd mentality can be harnessed for positive social change. This movement, which sought to end racial segregation and discrimination against African Americans, was characterized by widespread grassroots activism and nonviolent protest.

The movement was driven by a shared belief in the need for racial equality and justice, which was reinforced by the actions of others within the movement. The Montgomery Bus Boycott, sparked by Rosa Parks' refusal to give up her seat to a white passenger, is one of the most famous examples of this dynamic. Parks' defiance inspired thousands of others to join the boycott, which lasted over a year and ultimately led to the desegregation of public buses in Montgomery, Alabama.

The leadership of figures like Dr. Martin Luther King Jr. was also crucial in mobilizing the movement. King's eloquent speeches and commitment to nonviolence provided a unifying vision for the movement, rallying people nationwide to take action. The Civil Rights Movement achieved significant legal and social reforms, including the Civil Rights Act of 1964 and the Voting Rights Act of 1965.

The movement's success illustrates how herd mentality can lead to profound social change when guided by strong leadership and a clear moral vision. It also highlights the importance of collective action in challenging entrenched systems of power and oppression.

The Fall of the Berlin Wall (1989)

The fall of the Berlin Wall on November 9, 1989, is one of the most symbolic moments in modern history. It represented the end of the Cold War and the collapse of Communist regimes across Eastern Europe. The events leading up to the wall's fall were driven by a powerful social movement in East Germany, where citizens, tired of living under an oppressive regime, began to demand greater freedom and reform.

Throughout the 1980s, East Germany experienced growing economic difficulties, political repression, and a rising tide of discontent. Inspired by reforms in other Eastern Bloc countries, such as Poland's Solidarity movement, East Germans began to organize protests and demonstrations. The movement gained momentum in the autumn of 1989, with mass protests in cities like Leipzig, where tens of thousands took to the streets in what became known as the Monday Demonstrations.

As the protests grew, the East German government struggled to maintain control. The turning point came on November 9, 1989, when a government spokesman mistakenly announced that travel restrictions to the West would be lifted immediately. Thousands of East Berliners flocked to the Berlin Wall, and in the face of overwhelming numbers, the border guards stood down, allowing people to cross freely. The wall, a symbol of division for nearly three decades, was breached not by force but by the people's collective will.

The fall of the Berlin Wall marked the beginning of the end for the Communist regime in East Germany and led to the reunification of Germany the following year. This event underscores the power of collective action in bringing about political change, even in the face of seemingly insurmountable obstacles.

Conclusion: The Power and Peril of Herd Mentality in Social and Political Change

Social movements and political revolutions are among the most potent expressions of herd mentality. Throughout history, the collective behavior of individuals has driven significant social and political change, often in the face of formidable opposition. From the French Revolution to the Civil Rights Movement and the fall of the Berlin Wall, these examples illustrate both the power and the peril of herd mentality.

While herd mentality can lead to positive outcomes, such as expanding civil rights or overthrowing oppressive regimes, it can also result in chaos, violence, and unintended consequences. The same collective energy that drives a movement can, if not carefully managed, spiral out of control, leading to outcomes that deviate from the original goals.

As we continue to explore the dynamics of collective behavior in this book, it is essential to recognize that herd mentality is neither inherently good nor bad. It is a powerful force that can be harnessed for positive change, but it must be guided by strong leadership, a clear vision, and a commitment to justice and equality. Only then can we ensure that the power of the herd leads to progress rather than destruction.

Part IV: Resisting the Pull of the Herd

Chapter 8: The Importance of Critical Thinking

In a world where information is abundant and easily accessible, the ability to think critically has never been more critical. Whether we're navigating the complexities of social media, making decisions in our personal lives, or evaluating the credibility of news sources, critical thinking is the tool that helps us cut through the noise and arrive at sound conclusions. But what exactly is critical thinking, and why is it so crucial in resisting the powerful pull of herd mentality? In this chapter, we will explore the essence of critical thinking, the development of independent thought, and practical techniques to resist the often overwhelming influence of the crowd.

Developing Independent Thought

Critical thinking begins with developing independent thought—a process that requires curiosity, skepticism, and a willingness to challenge the status quo. Independent thinking is not about rejecting popular opinions; instead, it is about approaching information and situations with an open mind, evaluating evidence, and drawing conclusions based on rational analysis.

The Value of Curiosity

Curiosity is the foundation of independent thought. It drives us to ask questions, seek new information, and explore different perspectives. Albert Einstein once said, "The important thing is not to stop questioning. Curiosity has its reason for existing." In an age where information is often presented in bite-sized, easily digestible forms, curiosity compels us to dig deeper, to go beyond headlines and soundbites, and to understand the complexities of the issues at hand.

Developing curiosity involves cultivating a mindset that is always open to learning. This means seeking information confirming our beliefs and actively engaging with ideas that challenge our viewpoints. For example, someone curious about climate change might not only read articles that support their current understanding but also explore scientific papers, attend lectures, or engage in discussions with experts in the field.

Skepticism: A Healthy Dose of Doubt

While curiosity drives us to seek new information, skepticism ensures we do not accept everything at face value. Skepticism is questioning the validity of information, arguments, or assumptions. It is not about being cynical or distrustful but about applying a critical eye to the information we encounter.

In the context of resisting herd mentality, skepticism plays a crucial role. When everyone around us seems to adopt a particular belief or behavior, skepticism prompts us to ask: Why is this happening? What evidence supports this trend? Is there a possibility that this information is biased or incomplete? For instance, during the dot-com bubble of the late 1990s, a skeptical investor might have questioned the skyrocketing valuations of internet companies that had yet to turn a profit, thereby avoiding the financial losses many others experienced when the bubble burst.

The Courage to Stand Alone

Developing independent thought also requires the courage to stand alone and to hold on to one's convictions even when they go against the majority. This is perhaps the most challenging aspect of independent thinking, as humans are inherently social creatures who seek acceptance and validation from their peers.

History is replete with examples of individuals who dared to think independently, often at significant personal risk. Galileo Galilei, for instance, challenged the prevailing belief that the Earth was the center of the universe, advocating instead for the heliocentric model proposed by Copernicus. Despite facing persecution by the Catholic Church, Galileo's commitment to scientific truth laid the groundwork for modern astronomy.

Standing alone in the face of overwhelming consensus requires intellectual confidence and emotional resilience. It involves being comfortable with uncertainty, being willing to be wrong, and being prepared to change one's mind in the face of new evidence. This is the hallmark of a true critical thinker.

Techniques to Resist Herd Mentality

While developing independent thought is essential, it is equally important to have practical techniques to resist the powerful pull of herd mentality. In this section, we will explore strategies individuals can use to maintain their critical thinking skills, even in the face of overwhelming social pressure.

Questioning Assumptions

One of the most effective ways to resist herd mentality is to question the assumptions that underlie popular beliefs or behaviors consistently. This involves identifying the premises taken for granted and critically evaluating their validity.

For example, during the lead-up to the 2008 financial crisis, one widely held assumption was that housing prices would continue to rise indefinitely. This assumption was so deeply ingrained that it was largely unchallenged by investors and financial institutions. However, those who questioned this assumption and conducted their independent analysis were able to anticipate the collapse of the housing market and protect themselves from significant losses.

To practice questioning assumptions, individuals can ask themselves the following questions when encountering new information or trends:
- What assumptions are being made?
- Are these assumptions supported by evidence?
- What would happen if these assumptions were wrong?

By systematically questioning assumptions, individuals can uncover potential flaws in popular beliefs and make more informed decisions.

Seeking Out Diverse Perspectives

Another powerful technique for resisting herd mentality is to seek out diverse perspectives. This involves deliberately exposing oneself to a wide range of viewpoints, particularly those that differ from one's own. Engaging with different perspectives challenges cognitive biases and broadens our understanding of complex issues.

In practice, this might involve reading publications with different editorial stances, engaging in discussions with people with opposing views, or participating in forums encouraging debate and critical thinking. For example, someone interested in political issues might read conservative and liberal news sources, attend debates, and engage in discussions with individuals across the political spectrum.

Seeking diverse perspectives helps counteract the echo chamber effect and fosters empathy and understanding. It allows individuals to see issues from multiple angles and appreciate the complexities and nuances often overlooked in groupthink scenarios.

Slowing Down Decision-Making

Herd mentality often leads to hasty decision-making, driven by the fear of missing out or the pressure to conform.

To resist this, individuals can adopt the practice of slowing down their decision-making process. This involves taking the time to thoroughly evaluate options, gather information, and consider potential consequences before deciding.

For example, in financial markets, investors are often tempted to buy or sell assets quickly in response to market trends. However, by slowing down and conducting a thorough analysis, investors can avoid impulsive decisions and make more rational choices. This approach is also applicable in everyday life, whether making a significant purchase, deciding on a career move, or forming an opinion on a contentious issue.
Slowing decision-making allows individuals to engage in deeper reflection, reducing the likelihood of being swept up in the emotions or biases of the moment.

Building Critical Thinking Communities

Resisting herd mentality is more accessible when individuals are part of a community that values critical thinking and independent thought. Building or joining such communities can provide support, encouragement, and a space for open dialogue.

These communities can take many forms, from academic or professional groups to online forums and book clubs. The key is fostering an environment where questioning, debate, and exchanging ideas are encouraged. In these spaces, individuals can test their ideas, receive constructive feedback, and refine their thinking.

For example, the Socratic method, used in many educational settings, is a form of dialogue that encourages critical thinking through questioning and debate. Participants are asked to defend their ideas, respond to counterarguments, and think deeply about the issues. This method sharpens vital thinking skills and helps individuals become more comfortable with intellectual challenge and dissent.

Conclusion: The Path to True Independence

In a world where conformity often feels like the path of least resistance, the importance of critical thinking cannot be overstated. Developing independent thought and employing techniques to resist herd mentality is essential for navigating the complexities of modern life. Whether in politics, economics, or personal decision-making, thinking critically and independently is the key to making informed, rational choices.

As we have explored in this chapter, critical thinking is not a static skill but a dynamic process that requires curiosity, skepticism, and the courage to stand alone. It is a journey that involves questioning assumptions, seeking out diverse perspectives, slowing down decision-making, and building communities that value open dialogue.

By embracing these practices, individuals can break free from the constraints of herd mentality and chart their course, making decisions that are not just reactions to the crowd but reflections of careful, thoughtful analysis. In doing so, they contribute to a more informed, rational, and resilient society that values independent thought and the power of critical inquiry.

Conclusion

Chapter 9: Leadership and Influence

In times of crisis, uncertainty, or rapid change, people often look to leaders for guidance, reassurance, and direction. Leaders, whether heads of state, CEOs, activists, or influencers, possess the unique ability to shape and redirect the collective behavior of the groups they lead. The power of leadership lies not just in the ability to set a vision but in the capacity to influence the actions, beliefs, and attitudes of others. This chapter explores how leaders can harness the dynamics of herd behavior to achieve their goals, the ethical considerations they must navigate, and the profound impact their influence can have on society.

How Leaders Can Shape and Redirect the Herd

Leadership is as much about influence as it is about authority. While authority provides leaders with the formal power to make decisions, influence allows them to guide the thoughts and actions of their followers. Understanding the psychological underpinnings of herd behavior is crucial for leaders who seek to inspire collective action or shift the direction of a group.

The Power of Vision and Narrative

One of the most potent tools in a leader's arsenal is the ability to craft and communicate a compelling vision. A vision provides a sense of direction, a goal that unites the group and gives purpose to their collective efforts. Leaders like Martin Luther King Jr., who articulated a powerful vision of racial equality in his "I Have a Dream" speech, were able to mobilize large movements by painting a picture of a better future that resonated deeply with their followers.

Narratives play a central role in shaping collective behavior because they offer a framework through which people can understand their experiences and the world around them. A well-crafted narrative taps into shared values and emotions, making it easier for people to see themselves as part of a larger story. During the American Revolution, for example, leaders like Thomas Paine used powerful rhetoric in pamphlets like "Common Sense" to galvanize the colonists by framing their struggle for independence as a moral imperative.

Leaders who effectively use narratives to shape group behavior understand that people are not always driven by logic alone. Emotion, identity, and moral conviction are equally important drivers of behavior. By appealing to these elements through storytelling, leaders can align their followers' actions with their vision, creating a robust and cohesive group capable of significant collective action.

Leveraging Social Proof and Influence

Social proof, the psychological phenomenon where people look to others to determine their behavior, is another powerful tool for leaders. By strategically highlighting the actions of key individuals or groups, leaders can create a bandwagon effect, encouraging others to follow suit.

For example, during the early stages of the civil rights movement, leaders like Rosa Parks and Martin Luther King Jr. became symbols of resistance. Their actions provided social proof that standing up to injustice was possible and necessary, inspiring thousands of others to join the cause. Similarly, CEOs can use social proof in corporate environments by publicly endorsing certain behaviors, such as innovation or ethical practices, to set a standard others are likely to follow.

Leaders can also shape herd behavior by managing the flow of information. By controlling which messages are amplified and which are downplayed, leaders can influence the perceptions and priorities of their followers. In political campaigns, candidates often use targeted messaging to emphasize specific issues over others, guiding the public discourse and shaping voter behavior.

However, the use of social proof and influence comes with significant responsibility. While these techniques can effectively achieve positive outcomes, they can be misused to manipulate or deceive. Leaders must be mindful of the ethical implications of their influence and ensure that their actions serve the greater good rather than just their interests.

The Role of Charisma and Authority

Charisma is often cited as a critical characteristic of influential leaders. Charismatic leaders possess a magnetic personality that inspires loyalty and admiration. Their ability to communicate passionately and authentically can create a solid emotional connection with their followers, making rallying them around a cause easier.

Charismatic leaders like Nelson Mandela, who played a pivotal role in ending apartheid in South Africa, were able to unite people across diverse backgrounds by embodying the values and aspirations of their movements. Mandela's sacrifice, unwavering commitment to justice, and ability to forgive his oppressors made him a symbol of hope and reconciliation, inspiring millions to follow his lead.

Formal and informal authority also plays a crucial role in shaping herd behavior. Leaders who hold positions of power can leverage their authority to enforce rules, set standards, and guide behavior. However, the most influential leaders use their authority not to dominate but to empower others. By fostering an environment of trust, respect, and collaboration, leaders can encourage followers to take ownership of their collective goals and contribute to the group's success.

The use of charisma and authority in leadership requires a delicate balance. While these traits can inspire and mobilize, they can lead to blind obedience or the suppression of dissent if not checked by ethical considerations. Leaders must be aware of the potential for their influence to stifle critical thinking and ensure that they create space for diverse perspectives and constructive debate within their groups.

Ethical Considerations for Influencers

The ability to influence others is a powerful tool, but with great power comes great responsibility. Leaders and influencers must navigate a complex ethical landscape where the line between persuasion and manipulation can be thin. Their choices in how they wield their influence can have far-reaching consequences for their immediate followers and society.

The Ethics of Persuasion vs. Manipulation

At the heart of ethical leadership is the distinction between persuasion and manipulation. Persuasion guides others to a conclusion based on reason, evidence, and mutual respect. It involves presenting information honestly and allowing individuals to make informed decisions. Conversely, manipulation consists of misleading or coercing others to achieve a desired outcome, often at the expense of their autonomy or well-being.

For example, during World War II, propaganda was used extensively by both the Allies and the Axis powers to shape public opinion and boost morale. While propaganda can be a tool for persuasion, it often blurs the line into manipulation by selectively presenting information, appealing to emotions like fear or anger, and demonizing the enemy. Leaders who use such tactics must consider the ethical implications of their actions and the potential harm they may cause.

Ethical leaders prioritize transparency, honesty, and the welfare of their followers. They seek to empower others by giving them the tools and knowledge to make their own decisions rather than simply dictating their choices. In doing so, they build trust and create a culture of integrity within their organizations or movements.

The Responsibility to Foster Critical Thinking

One key responsibility of ethical leaders is to foster critical thinking among their followers. While it may be tempting to encourage conformity and unity, authentic leadership involves cultivating an environment where questioning and dissent are valued. This not only strengthens the group by exposing it to diverse perspectives but also helps prevent the dangers of groupthink and blind obedience.

Leaders can foster critical thinking by encouraging open dialogue, inviting feedback, and creating opportunities for learning and growth. In the corporate world, for example, companies like Google and Amazon have institutionalized practices that encourage employees to challenge assumptions and think creatively. By creating a culture that values critical thinking, these companies have been able to foster innovation and stay ahead in competitive markets.

Fostering critical thinking is equally important in political and social movements. Leaders who encourage their followers to question authority, consider alternative viewpoints, and engage in informed debate are more likely to build sustainable, resilient movements that adapt to changing circumstances. This approach also helps protect against the risks of authoritarianism and the concentration of power in the hands of a few.

Balancing Influence with Autonomy

A fundamental ethical consideration for leaders is balancing their influence with their followers' autonomy. While leaders have a role in guiding and inspiring collective action, they must also respect the individual agency of those they lead. This means avoiding coercive tactics, allowing space for personal choice, and ensuring that followers are fully informed.

This balance is particularly relevant to digital influencers. Social media influencers wield significant power over their audiences, often shaping trends, opinions, and purchasing decisions. However, their ethical responsibility includes being transparent about sponsored content, avoiding promoting harmful products, and respecting the diversity of their followers' needs and preferences.

For example, when the "influencer economy" boomed in the mid-2010s, many influencers faced backlash for promoting ineffective or harmful products, such as unproven diet supplements. Ethical influencers responded by becoming more transparent about their endorsements, choosing to promote only products they genuinely believed in, and prioritizing the well-being of their followers over profit.

Conclusion: The Ethical Imperative of Leadership

Leadership is a powerful force in shaping the behavior and beliefs of groups, but with that power comes a profound ethical responsibility. Leaders who understand the dynamics of herd behavior can use their influence to inspire positive change, guide their followers toward shared goals, and build stronger, more resilient communities. However, their methods—whether through vision, narrative, social proof, or authority—must be tempered by a commitment to ethical principles.

As we have explored in this chapter, the line between persuasion and manipulation is often fine, and the consequences of crossing it can be significant. Ethical leaders prioritize transparency, foster critical thinking, and respect the autonomy of their followers. By doing so, they achieve their goals and contribute to the greater good, ensuring their influence is used to uplift rather than exploit.

Appendices

Appendix A: Key Terms and Concepts

In understanding the intricate dynamics of herd behavior and collective psychology, one must familiarize oneself with key terms and concepts that frequently arise throughout the study of these phenomena. This appendix provides clear, concise definitions and explanations of the most critical concepts discussed in the book. These terms will serve as a reference point for readers, helping to clarify the complex ideas that underpin the psychology of collective behavior.

Herd Mentality

Definition: Herd mentality, also known as mob mentality or pack mentality, refers to the tendency of individuals to conform to the actions, behaviors, or opinions of a larger group, often overriding their own judgment or rational thought.
Example: During the 1929 stock market crash, investors, driven by the fear of missing out and seeing others selling their stocks, also began to sell off their shares, exacerbating the market decline.
Relevance: Understanding herd mentality is crucial in examining how group dynamics can influence individual decisions, leading to collective actions that may not align with individual best interests.

Social Proof

Definition: Social proof is a psychological and social phenomenon in which people assume the actions of others in an attempt to reflect correct behavior in a given situation. This concept is based on the idea that individuals are more likely to follow the behavior of the masses when they are unsure of what to do.

Example: In marketing, products labeled as "best sellers" or "most popular" often attract more buyers because people tend to trust the choices made by others.

Relevance: Social proof plays a significant role in herd behavior, as it reinforces the idea that if many people are doing something, it must be the right thing to do.

Groupthink

Definition: Groupthink is a psychological phenomenon that occurs within a group of people when the desire for harmony or conformity in the group results in an irrational or dysfunctional decision-making outcome. Group members often suppress dissenting opinions, leading to a consensus that may not reflect the best possible decision.

Example: The Bay of Pigs invasion is a classic example of groupthink. Despite having reservations, U.S. government officials went along with a flawed plan due to the pressure to conform to the group's consensus.

Relevance: Groupthink is critical in understanding how cohesive groups can sometimes make poor decisions by prioritizing consensus over critical evaluation of alternatives.

Information Cascade

Definition: An information cascade occurs when individuals make decisions based on the observations or actions of others rather than their private information. This can lead to a rapid spread of behaviors or beliefs, often without thorough evaluation of the information.

Example: During the early stages of the COVID-19 pandemic, panic buying of toilet paper became an information cascade as people saw others stockpiling and assumed they should do the same, leading to widespread shortages.

Relevance: Information cascades illustrate how quickly and pervasively certain behaviors or beliefs can spread through a population, especially in the digital age where information is disseminated rapidly.

Cognitive Biases

Definition: Cognitive biases are systematic patterns of deviation from norm or rationality in judgment. They often arise from the brain's attempt to simplify information processing and can lead to errors in thinking, particularly in group settings.

Example: Confirmation bias, where individuals favor information that confirms their pre-existing beliefs, can lead to distorted decision-making, especially in politically charged environments.

Relevance: Understanding cognitive biases is essential for identifying how collective behavior can sway individual thinking and developing strategies to mitigate these effects.

Anchoring Bias

Definition: Anchoring bias occurs when individuals rely too heavily on an initial piece of information (the "anchor") when making decisions, even when subsequent information should carry more weight.

Example: In negotiations, the first number discussed often serves as an anchor, heavily influencing the final agreement, regardless of its accuracy or fairness.

Relevance: Anchoring bias is particularly relevant in financial markets and negotiations, where initial information can disproportionately shape outcomes.

Bandwagon Effect

Definition: The bandwagon effect is the tendency of people to adopt certain behaviors, styles, or attitudes simply because others are doing so. This effect is closely related to herd mentality and social proof.

Example: The sudden rise in the popularity of fidget spinners in 2017 is an example of the bandwagon effect, where the product's popularity soared because so many people were buying and using them.

Relevance: The bandwagon effect helps explain how trends and fads emerge and why certain behaviors or products can suddenly become widespread.

Echo Chamber

Definition: An echo chamber is an environment where people only encounter information or opinions that reflect and reinforce their own, often due to the selective exposure enabled by social media algorithms.

Example: On social media platforms, users are often shown content that aligns with their existing views, which can

create a distorted sense of consensus and discourage exposure to diverse perspectives.
Relevance: Echo chambers are significant in the context of political polarization and the spread of misinformation, as they can intensify groupthink and reduce critical engagement with opposing viewpoints.

Confirmation Bias
Definition: Confirmation bias is the tendency to search for, interpret, and remember information in a way that confirms one's pre-existing beliefs or values while giving less consideration to alternative possibilities.
Example: During a political debate, a person may only focus on arguments that support their preferred candidate, ignoring valid points made by the opposition.
Relevance: Confirmation bias is a powerful cognitive bias that can reinforce herd behavior by leading individuals to process information that aligns with the dominant group opinion selectively.

Moral Panic
Definition: Moral panic refers to the intense feeling of fear spread among a large number of people that some evil threatens society's well-being. It often leads to a surge in public and media concern, followed by a governmental response.
Example: The Red Scare in the United States during the 1950s, characterized by the fear of communist infiltration, led to widespread paranoia, blacklisting, and the McCarthy hearings.
Relevance: Moral panics are significant in understanding how media and societal fears can lead to exaggerated

perceptions of threat, influencing public opinion and policy in ways that actual risks may not justify.

Mass Hysteria
Definition: Mass hysteria, or collective hysteria, is a phenomenon in which people exhibit similar hysterical symptoms, often involving irrational fears or beliefs, and spread rapidly through a population.
Example: The Salem Witch Trials in 1692, where a group of young girls in Salem, Massachusetts, claimed to be possessed by the devil, leading to a wave of hysteria and the execution of 20 people accused of witchcraft.
Relevance: Mass hysteria is a stark example of how herd behavior can lead to irrational and dangerous actions fueled by fear and the reinforcement of group beliefs.

Leader-Follower Dynamics
Definition: Leader-follower dynamics refer to the relationships and interactions between leaders and their followers, where leaders exert influence and followers respond, often leading to coordinated group action.
Example: During World War II, Winston Churchill's speeches and leadership were instrumental in rallying the British people during the Blitz, providing hope and resilience in the face of adversity.
Relevance: Understanding leader-follower dynamics is crucial for analyzing how leaders can guide, inspire, or manipulate groups, shaping collective behavior.

Appendix B: Recommended Reading and Resources

Understanding the psychology of collective behavior and herd mentality requires delving into various disciplines, from psychology and sociology to history and economics. The following recommended readings and resources have been carefully selected to provide readers with a deeper understanding of the topics covered in this book. These works offer valuable insights, case studies, and theoretical frameworks that can help further explore the dynamics of group behavior, influence, and leadership. Whether you're a scholar, student, or curious reader, these resources will enrich your understanding of the complex forces that drive human behavior in groups.

1. *Influence: The Psychology of Persuasion* **by Robert Cialdini**
Summary: Robert Cialdini's *Influence* is a seminal work that explores the psychological principles behind why people say "yes" and how others influence them. Cialdini identifies six fundamental principles of influence — reciprocity, commitment, social proof, authority, liking, and scarcity — and explains how these principles can be leveraged to persuade others.
Why It's Recommended: This book provides a comprehensive look at the mechanisms of social influence, which are central to understanding herd behavior. Cialdini's work is precious for its practical insights, making it accessible to academic audiences and those interested in applying these principles in real-world scenarios.

2. *The Crowd: A Study of the Popular Mind* **by Gustave Le Bon**
Summary: Gustave Le Bon's *The Crowd* is a classic exploration of the psychology of crowds and how individuals in groups can exhibit behaviors different from their everyday actions when alone. Le Bon argues that crowds are governed by a "collective mind" that leads to irrational and emotional behavior, often with significant social and political consequences.

Why It's Recommended: Le Bon's work is foundational in studying collective behavior and remains relevant today. His insights into the dynamics of crowds offer a historical perspective on how group behavior can influence events such as revolutions, social movements, and even financial markets.

3. *Thinking, Fast and Slow* **by Daniel Kahneman**
Summary: Nobel laureate Daniel Kahneman's *Thinking, Fast and Slow* delves into the dual processes that drive our thinking: the fast, intuitive, and emotional system and the slower, more deliberate, and logical system. Kahneman explores how these systems interact and how they often lead to cognitive biases that affect our decisions and judgments.

Why It's Recommended: Kahneman's exploration of cognitive biases is crucial for understanding the psychological underpinnings of herd mentality. The book offers deep insights into how individuals process information and make decisions and how the behavior of others can influence these processes.

4. *Extraordinary Popular Delusions and the Madness of Crowds* **by Charles Mackay**

Summary: First published in 1841, Charles Mackay's *Extraordinary Popular Delusions and the Madness of Crowds* examines historical mass hysteria, economic bubbles, and other instances where collective behavior has led to irrational and sometimes destructive outcomes. Mackay's work covers a range of phenomena, from the Dutch Tulip Mania to the South Sea Bubble.

Why It's Recommended: Mackay's work is one of the earliest studies on the irrationality of crowds and offers a fascinating look at how herd behavior has manifested throughout history. It is an essential read for anyone interested in collective behavior's economic and social aspects.

5. *The Wisdom of Crowds* **by James Surowiecki**

Summary: In *The Wisdom of Crowds*, James Surowiecki argues that under the right conditions, groups can make better decisions than individuals, even when the group includes non-experts. He explores the factors contributing to successful group decision-making and the situations where collective intelligence outperforms individual judgment.

Why It's Recommended: Surowiecki's book counters the often negative perceptions of herd mentality, demonstrating that collective behavior can be beneficial when structured correctly. This work is particularly relevant for those interested in the potential of collective intelligence in decision-making processes.

6. *The Power of Habit: Why We Do What We Do in Life and Business* **by Charles Duhigg**
Summary: Charles Duhigg's *The Power of Habit* explores the science of habits—how they are formed, can be changed, and influence individual and group behavior. Duhigg examines how habits play a role in business, social movements, and daily life, offering insights into how they can be harnessed for positive change.

Why It's Recommended: Understanding habits is crucial to understanding how group behaviors are formed and reinforced. Duhigg's exploration of habit formation provides valuable insights into how leaders and organizations can influence collective behavior by creating new habits.

7. *Nudge: Improving Decisions About Health, Wealth, and Happiness* **by Richard H. Thaler and Cass R. Sunstein**
Summary: *Nudge* by Richard Thaler and Cass Sunstein explores how small changes in how choices are presented—referred to as "nudges"—can significantly impact decision-making and behavior. The authors argue that well-designed nudges can help people make better decisions without restricting their freedom of choice.

Why It's Recommended: This book is particularly relevant for understanding how subtle influences can shape collective behavior. Thaler and Sunstein's concept of "nudging" offers practical applications for policymakers, leaders, and anyone interested in ethically guiding group behavior.

8. *Blink: The Power of Thinking Without Thinking* **by Malcolm Gladwell**

Summary: In *Blink*, Malcolm Gladwell explores the power of quick, intuitive decisions and how they can be incredibly effective and dangerously flawed. Gladwell examines the role of rapid cognition in various contexts, from military strategy to art criticism, and the factors that influence these snap judgments.

Why It's Recommended: *Blink* provides insights into the unconscious processes that drive decision-making, often at play in herd behavior. Gladwell's exploration of intuition complements the broader study of how individuals and groups make decisions, particularly in high-pressure situations.

9. *Sapiens: A Brief History of Humankind* **by Yuval Noah Harari**

Summary: Yuval Noah Harari's *Sapiens* offers a sweeping history of humanity, exploring how Homo sapiens came to dominate the world. Harari examines the cognitive revolution, the development of cultures, and the rise of nations, all through the lens of collective human behavior.

Why It's Recommended: *Sapiens* provides a broader context for understanding how collective behavior has shaped human history. Harari's exploration of shared myths, cultures, and ideologies offers valuable insights into the foundations of herd behavior and its impact on the development of civilizations.

10. *Switch: How to Change Things When Change Is Hard* **by Chip Heath and Dan Heath**
Summary: In *Switch*, Chip and Dan Heath explore the psychology of change and the factors that make it difficult for individuals and organizations to adopt new behaviors. The authors provide a framework for understanding how to create lasting change by appealing to both the rational and emotional sides of human decision-making.

Why It's Recommended: *Switch* is handy for leaders, educators, and anyone interested in influencing group behavior. The Heath brothers' practical strategies for driving change directly apply to efforts to steer herd behavior in positive directions.

Additional Resources

1. The Behavioral Economics Guide
Website: www.behavioraleconomics.com Summary: This comprehensive guide provides an overview of key concepts in behavioral economics, including cognitive biases, decision-making, and social influence. The site offers articles, research papers, and resources for further study.

2. The Greater Good Science Center
Website: greatergood.berkeley.edu Summary: The Greater Good Science Center at UC Berkeley explores the psychology of well-being and social behavior. Their resources include articles, podcasts, and research on empathy, altruism, and collective behavior.

3. TED Talks

Website: www.ted.com Summary: TED Talks offers a vast collection of presentations by experts in various fields, including psychology, leadership, and social behavior. Talks such as "The Power of Vulnerability" by Brené Brown and "How to Start a Movement" by Derek Sivers are particularly relevant to the study of herd behavior and leadership.

4. Coursera and edX

Websites: www.coursera.org, www.edx.org Summary: These online learning platforms offer courses on various topics, including psychology, sociology, and leadership. Courses such as "The Science of Well-Being" by Yale University on Coursera and "Behavioral Economics in Action" by the University of Toronto on edX are valuable resources for those looking to deepen their understanding of the concepts discussed in this book.

Conclusion

This appendix provides a curated selection of books and resources that will help you delve deeper into herd behavior, collective psychology, and leadership. Each recommendation has been chosen for its relevance, accessibility, and potential to enrich your understanding of how human behavior is shaped by the groups we belong to. Whether you're looking to expand your knowledge, gain practical insights, or explore these fascinating subjects further, these readings and resources offer a wealth of information to guide your journey.

Appendix C: Case Study Analysis

In exploring the complexities of herd behavior and collective psychology, case studies provide a crucial window into real-world applications of these concepts. We can better understand how social influence, group dynamics, and leadership theories manifest in practical scenarios through detailed analysis of specific events. This appendix offers a deep dive into several case studies that illustrate the power of herd behavior in various contexts — from financial markets to social movements. Each case study is analyzed to highlight the key factors that drove collective behavior, the outcomes, and the lessons that can be drawn from these events.

Case Study 1: The Dot-Com Bubble (1995-2000)

Background and Context

The Dot-Com Bubble of the late 1990s is one of the most dramatic examples of herd behavior in financial markets. As the internet emerged as a transformative technology, investors poured money into technology companies, particularly those associated with the burgeoning Internet sector. The frenzy was fueled by the belief that the internet would revolutionize the economy, leading to an unprecedented rise in stock valuations for companies that were often little more than a website and a business plan.

The Role of Herd Behavior

Herd behavior was central to the rapid inflation of the dot-com bubble. Investors, driven by the fear of missing out (FOMO) and the bandwagon effect, rushed to buy shares in internet companies, driving prices to astronomical levels. Social proof also played a significant role, with the actions of influential investors and analysts reinforcing the perception that these companies were sound investments. Media coverage further amplified this effect, creating a feedback loop where rising stock prices attracted more investors, pushing prices even higher.

Outcome and Consequences

The bubble burst in March 2000, leading to a massive sell-off in technology stocks. The NASDAQ Composite, which had soared to over 5,000 points, plummeted by nearly 80% over the next two years. Many dot-com companies went bankrupt, and trillions of dollars in market value were wiped out. The aftermath of the crash had a lasting impact on the economy, leading to a recession and shaking investor confidence in the technology sector.

Lessons Learned

The Dot-Com Bubble illustrates the dangers of herd behavior in financial markets, particularly when it is driven by speculative fervor rather than sound economic analysis. It also underscores the importance of critical thinking and due diligence in investment decisions. Investors who could resist the herd mentality and focus on fundamentals were better positioned to avoid the catastrophic losses that followed the bubble's burst.

Case Study 2: The Salem Witch Trials (1692)

Background and Context

The Salem Witch Trials, which took place in colonial Massachusetts between 1692 and 1693, represent one of the most infamous episodes of mass hysteria in American history. The trials were sparked by a group of young girls in Salem Village who claimed to be possessed by the devil and accused several local women of witchcraft. The accusations quickly spread, leading to a series of trials and the execution of 20 people.

The Role of Herd Behavior

Herd behavior was a driving force behind the rapid escalation of the witch trials. The fear of witchcraft, coupled with the intense social pressures of the time, led the community to accept the accusations as truth quickly. The bandwagon effect was evident as more and more people came forward with allegations, often motivated by personal grudges or the desire to conform to the prevailing narrative. The groupthink phenomenon also played a role, as dissenting voices were silenced or ignored in the face of overwhelming consensus.

Outcome and Consequences

The Salem Witch Trials resulted in the execution of 20 people and the imprisonment of many others. The hysteria eventually subsided as doubts about the validity of the trials grew, and public opinion began to turn against the proceedings. The trials left a lasting legacy of shame and regret, and they are now seen as a cautionary tale about the dangers of mass hysteria and the consequences of abandoning due process.

Lessons Learned

The Salem Witch Trials highlight the destructive potential of herd behavior when it is fueled by fear and superstition. They also demonstrate the importance of maintaining a fair and rational legal process, even under public pressure. The trials serve as a reminder of the need to protect individual rights and to resist the temptation to scapegoat others during times of crisis.

Case Study 3: The Arab Spring (2010-2011)

Background and Context

The Arab Spring was a series of anti-government protests, uprisings, and armed rebellions that spread across much of the Arab world in the early 2010s. The movement began in Tunisia in December 2010, following the self-immolation of a street vendor in protest against police corruption and ill-treatment. This desperation sparked a wave of demonstrations that quickly spread to other countries, including Egypt, Libya, Syria, and Yemen.

The Role of Herd Behavior

Herd behavior was a critical factor in the rapid spread of the Arab Spring across the region. Social media platforms like Facebook and Twitter were crucial in mobilizing protesters and spreading information, creating a sense of collective identity and shared purpose among disparate groups. The bandwagon effect was evident as the success of protests in one country inspired similar actions in others, leading to a domino effect across the region. The desire for social proof also drove the movement, as individuals were motivated to join the protests when they saw others doing the same.

Outcome and Consequences

The Arab Spring overthrew several long-standing authoritarian regimes, including those of Tunisia's Zine El Abidine Ben Ali, Egypt's Hosni Mubarak, and Libya's Muammar Gaddafi. However, the outcomes were mixed, with some countries, like Tunisia, transitioning to democracy while others, like Syria, descended into civil war. The movement also had far-reaching consequences for the region's geopolitical landscape, leading to ongoing instability and conflict in several countries.

Lessons Learned

The Arab Spring demonstrates the power of herd behavior in driving social and political change. It also highlights the role of modern communication technologies in facilitating collective action. However, the varied outcomes of the Arab Spring underscore the complexity of social movements and the challenges of translating popular uprisings into lasting political change. The case study serves as a reminder of the importance of leadership, strategy, and vision in guiding movements toward successful outcomes.

Case Study 4: The COVID-19 Pandemic and Mask-Wearing (2020-2021)

Background and Context
The COVID-19 pandemic, which began in late 2019, quickly became a global health crisis, prompting governments worldwide to implement measures to slow the spread of the virus. One of the most visible and controversial measures was the recommendation or mandate for people to wear masks in public settings. The issue of mask-wearing became highly politicized, leading to divisions within societies and varying levels of compliance.

The Role of Herd Behavior

Herd behavior played a significant role in adopting and rejecting mask-wearing. In some communities, the early adoption of masks by influential figures and public health officials led to widespread acceptance and compliance. Social proof reinforced the behavior, as people saw others wearing masks and followed suit. However, in other communities, resistance to mask-wearing was fueled by political leaders and media figures who downplayed the severity of the virus or framed mask mandates as an infringement on personal freedom. This led to a counter-bandwagon effect, where individuals who identified with these leaders refused to wear masks, often citing the actions of others in their group as justification.

Outcome and Consequences

The varied response to mask-wearing had significant public health implications. In regions where mask-wearing was widely adopted, the spread of the virus was more effectively controlled, reducing the strain on healthcare systems. Conversely, higher transmission rates and more severe outbreaks were often observed in areas where mask-wearing was resisted. The politicization of mask-wearing also contributed to social divisions and conflict, complicating efforts to achieve a coordinated public health response.

Lessons Learned

The case of mask-wearing during the COVID-19 pandemic illustrates how herd behavior can be influenced by political and cultural factors, leading to divergent outcomes in different communities. It also highlights the importance of clear and consistent messaging from leaders and public health officials in shaping collective behavior during a crisis. The case study serves as a reminder of the power of social influence in public health and the need for strategies that consider different groups' diverse motivations and beliefs.

Conclusion

The case studies presented in this appendix offer a rich exploration of how herd behavior manifests in different contexts, from financial markets to social movements and public health crises. Each case provides valuable insights into the factors that drive collective behavior, the outcomes of such behavior, and the lessons that can be drawn to inform future actions.

By examining these real-world examples, we gain a deeper understanding of the complex interplay between individual decision-making and group dynamics. These case studies also underscore the importance of leadership, communication, and critical thinking in guiding collective behavior toward positive outcomes. As we continue to study the psychology of herd behavior, these historical and contemporary examples will serve as important reference points for understanding the power and potential of collective action.

Dave Karpinsky, PhD, MBA, PMP, is a globally recognized consultant, executive leader, and professional author whose work bridges business transformation, strategy, and personal development. With over three decades of experience advising Fortune 500 companies, government agencies, and high-growth startups where he traveled to more than 60 countries, Dave brings a rare blend of practical insight, operational excellence, and visionary thinking to every project—and every page.

His career spans top-tier consulting firms including McKinsey & Company, Accenture, SAP, Cognizant, BearingPoint, Ernst & Young, Infosys, and IBM. He has led multi-million-dollar strategic and technology initiatives for global leaders such as Capital One, Coca-Cola, Costco, DHS/TSA, Google, HP, Janus Henderson, John Deere, Lockheed Martin, McLaren, Merck, Nike, PetSmart, QuidelOrtho, and ViaSat, as well as large-scale public sector programs for the US Government, States of Alaska, Arizona, California, Florida, and Georgia.

As the author of numerous books on project turnaround, leadership, SAP implementation, and personal mastery, Dave is known for translating complex challenges into actionable strategies that deliver measurable impact. His writing combines analytical precision with compelling storytelling—whether he's decoding enterprise system failures or exploring the psychological dynamics of decision-making and influence.

Dave holds advanced degrees in business, technology and psychology, along with a portfolio of elite professional certifications. He is a sought-after speaker, strategist, and transformation advisor who empowers individuals and organizations to break through barriers and unlock lasting success.

Outside of his professional pursuits, Dave is an avid traveler and photographer, with a passion for astrophotography and a curated collection of high-performance and exotic cars. His global perspective, intellectual curiosity, and relentless drive to improve systems and people continue to inspire readers and clients alike.

To my constant joy and loyal hearts – you make life lighter

"Civilization advanced when someone broke away from the herd—not when they blended into it."
— *Dave Karpinsky*

www.ingramcontent.com/pod-product-compliance
Lightning Source LLC
Chambersburg PA
CBHW020503030426
42337CB00011B/211